ENDORSE~~MENTS~~

If you've heard even a third of Andy Mason's story, you know how gutsy he is. He's beyond gutsy—he's mercenary! But he's not Wall-Street mercenary. Andy is mercenary about proving God loves entrepreneurs and business. The Kingdom is open for business 24/7/365, and Andy's got the stories to prove it. If you've never been certain that God wants to break into your world and rock your business...if you've built your business with one foot on the gas and one foot on the brake because you didn't possess total conviction that business success is a holy pursuit... you need this book. Great opportunities abound for entrepreneurs, marketers and salespeople, yet political and economic turmoil threaten us. Here, Andy demonstrates that the wisdom and generosity of God overcome all.

Perry Marshall
Bestselling author of *80/20 Sales & Marketing* and
The Ultimate Guide to Google AdWords

God With You at Work will inspire, encourage, and equip you to new levels of partnering with God in the marketplace that you never imagined possible. This book is a training manual for followers of Christ to impart a clear understanding of their calling, anointing and focus and to view their careers as their primary expression for building God's kingdom. It will help equip marketplace believers to become spiritual and natural leaders, establishing the Kingdom of God in every sphere of influence. If you are longing to get equipped with supernatural power in order to see societies transformed, then this book is for you!

Kris Vallotton
Senior Associate Leader, Bethel Church, California, USA
Co-Founder of Bethel School of Supernatural Ministry
Author of *The Supernatural Ways of Royalty* and *Spirit Wars*

Many people have swallowed the lie that they are to leave the Kingdom of God at the front door when they walk into work and pick it up again on the way out. As a result they operate like a non-voting representative of the Kingdom for a quarter of their lives. It is made worse by being brought up to think that the ultimate calling is that of full-time ministry and that somehow pastors and ministers are more holy, more powerful and more anointed with power than other professions or jobs. Andy's new book blows these lies away with a pragmatic exploration of why and how the power of the Kingdom of Jesus is available in the workplace for all who believe. With fantastic testimonies, an easy-to-read style and chapter-by-chapter suggestions to take action, this is a must-read book for anyone wanting to see God expand His Kingdom. Whether you make coffee or design rockets you need to read this book and see the release of His power into a new frontier of influence, the workplace.

Bruce Heesterman
CEO, Wellington, New Zealand

What if the same God of Joseph, Daniel and all the other heroes of the bible, who accomplished extraordinary tasks in the marketplace, would show up through us? Without a doubt, it would blow our wildest dreams. We live in a time where more believers in Christ cover the earth, than in all the centuries before us. God is eager to partner with us. To do that more effectively we have to know what we can do to eliminate the obstacles that hinder us from partnering with Him. In *God With You at Work*, Andy challenges us to think from a kingdom perspective, giving us the encouragement and the tools to accomplish the task. The way he conducts his own life is a true example of everything he talks about in this book.

The best testimonies of releasing God's glory come from lives that radiate a willingness to let the Fathers love infiltrate every aspect of our personality. This book fills a gap, enabling us to build the right foundation to bring the Kingdom of freedom to the marketplace.

Klaus & Suzy Merg
Merg & More Consultants, Germany

"Without vision, people perish." In *God With You at Work*, Andy delivers the antidote for lack of vision in the workplace. He takes you through a practical journey of knowing who you are and Whose you are as he brilliantly lays out this book with practical applications at the end of each chapter that will cause the reader to be challenged and poised for growth. His passion shines through in his personal testimony coupled with personal breakthrough of various business leaders.

By the end of this book, you will be supercharged with the Power of God through the Power of Testimony. I had always seen God's Hand on me in the workplace, but after attending a Heaven in Business workshop and reading both Dream Culture and now *God With You at Work*, it has inspired me to expect my workplace to be transformed by the Power of God, to see His Kingdom come in my workplace as it is in Heaven.

Brent Daldo
VP of Operations, ASC Industries Inc., Ohio, USA

What does it look like for Heaven to touch down on a business? Bethel Church has given such a gift to the Body of Christ in pioneering the way for the supernatural Presence of God to invade our churches, our streets and our homes. Andy Mason is taking this to another realm by demonstrating how God can show up in our businesses and workplaces as well. This book shows how God loves to partner with people in business, bringing new levels of excellence, creativity and innovation to the solutions people need. From heart foundations through to practical outworking, *God With You at Work* will encourage every businessperson to believe for and experience more of Heaven invading their world.

Tim Ferris
Director, The Leadership Resource, Sydney, Australia

As a medical doctor, I know the challenges of integrating my faith into my workplace. I have found such joy and peace as I have done so, and have seen the lives of my colleagues and patients enriched by the love and power of God at work through me. Through *God With You at Work* Andy can help you know how to integrate the secrets of the kingdom of God into your everyday life, and also enable you to dream and trust for bigger and greater things.

Dr. Pete Carter MB ChB
General practitioner, Kent, England
Author of *Unwrapping Lazarus*

"In Exodus 33:16, Moses asks The Lord, "How will anyone one know that you are pleased with your people unless you go with us? What else will distinguish me and your people from all the other people on the face of the earth?" In *God With You at Work*, Andy paints a picture of what looks like in business today.

God With You at Work is honest, challenging, practical and very encouraging. Andy answers the question many of us have asked, but few have dared to explore: "What would happen if we invited the fullness of who God is into our business?" By sharing his own story and those of others, we are given an idea of the 'distinguishing nature of God's presence' manifest in practical ways in the lives of so many men and women in business.

God With You at Work is a must-read for all who desire to encounter God in a very practical way. What you will discover in this book can be applied in every area of your life.

Juan Swart
General Manager, The Hartley Group, Kansas City, USA

Andy Mason is a catalyst for positive growth and giant-picture thinking. If your dreams are big, get ready for them to be huge! If your city is in your heart, get ready for the nations! Andy brings out the gold in people and inspires them to experience their potential in life. I whole-heartedly recommend this book to anyone hungry to lay hold of all that Christ laid hold of them for.

Philip Licht
Executive Director, Set Free Alaska, USA

Do you desire to transfer and release the life-altering revelations and encounters with God from your closet prayer time into your workplace? The book you hold in your hands is the key to making your desire a practical reality. *God With You at Work* guides you every step of the way by utilizing education (the Bible), revelation (thought-provoking questions) and implementation (activation exercises). This book is not meant to be just read; it's meant to become a lifestyle.

God With You at Work is much more than a book. It is the result of a reformative movement called Heaven in Business that Andy Mason has pioneered. The movement is breaking down the barriers in individuals and organizations that have held back the progress of God from invading the workplace. All the principles shared in the book are being practiced by a growing community. Read this book, answer the questions it asks you and then dare to accept the invitation to bring "God With You at Work." God is ready and willing; all you need to do is accept His invitation. If you say yes, be prepared to be swept up into something much bigger than yourself and better than you could imagine. The choice is yours.

David Charlson
Product and Business Developer, Radio Systems Corporation
California, USA

Andy's new book *God with You at Work* provokes our mindsets to shift from business-as-usual to a no-holds barred, Spirit-infused realm of dunamis power. With riveting testimonies, dynamic application and compelling wisdom packed in its pages, *God with You at Work* is a must read for those ravenous to uncork God's manifest goodness in all aspects of life. As co-laborers, we get the joy of taking this partnership to a realm bound only by imagination. By the time you're done with this book, you will be so convinced there's only one-way to live: fearlessly and audaciously, with God.

Jenn Co
Media Host and Producer, Vancouver, Canada

Behind every beautiful painting is an artist. However, it is not unusual to know more about the painting than the artist. *God With You at Work* is similar to a beautiful painting. It brings to life the possibility of living from the Presence of God in your workplace. More importantly, the book powerfully communicates the heart and passion of the author, Andy Mason. I have personally partnered with Andy at each Heaven in Business conference to date, and when Andy speaks or writes, I listen! Read this book and you will be forever encouraged and challenged, but you will also see the heart of the man behind the book. Welcome to the revolution of Heaven in your business!

Doug Hignell
Chairman of Board, The Hignell Companies, California, USA

The power of the testimony and the idea of performance from a place of rest, are two catalytic central themes in Andy Mason's newest book, *God With You at Work*. Throughout the book Andy weaves in testimonies of God 'showing up' with amazing miracles in the most unlikely circumstances. These powerful testimonies will be a basis for renewing our minds on what is possible and asking the Lord to 'do it again' in our own businesses.

The idea of performance from rest will draw the performers—those who believe God needs our work—into a revelation of the intimacy He desires with us above all. God placed the dreams for business in our hearts and wants us to seek Him as our business partner. We get to access strategies from God's very throne room, living from intimacy, connection and a confident dependence on Him.

Thank you, Andy, for the testimonies and the revelation shared in this book and for your heart to impact lives for God's kingdom!

Deanna Cannon, CPA
Executive Director, Northern Michigan Angels, USA
President and Co-Founder, Cannon & Company CPAs PLC, USA

HEAVEN IN BUSINESS
SERIES

GOD
WITH YOU AT WORK

ANDY MASON

Heaven in Business Series
GOD WITH YOU AT WORK

Cover design by Brad Webster, websterbranding.com
Interior design by Jonathan McGraw, jonathanmcgraw.net
Author's photo by Tracey Hedge, FireflyMobileStudio.com

ISBN-13:978:1492264378
ISBN-10:1492264377

To order more books or resources contact
info@HeavenInBusiness.com

CONTENTS

ACKNOWLEDGMENTS

I've heard it said if you see a turtle on top of a fence post, it didn't get there by itself. True! I want to acknowledge some of the people who have been a part of my journey in putting this work together.

Thanks Danny Silk for being the greatest example of an empowering leader I have ever personally experienced. You provided me an environment for this experiment to begin. Without your belief in me, this would not have happened. Enjoy the fruit of it!

Thanks to my team of advisors, encouragers and partners on this journey to co-labor with more of God in the marketplace. The view from your shoulders is awesome. Thanks for lending me your strength and allowing me to lean on your wisdom, experience and practical help. Rick and Linda Sbrocca, Mike and Robbie Frank, Dennis and Shelly Wade, Doug Hignell, Blake and Linda Schellenberg, Eric and Sadie Hess, Shain and Nisa Zumbrunnen, and most of all the wise and beautiful Janine Mason.

Thanks to my local Heaven in Business team, who carry so much of what we are doing in living out this message in our own city. Tim Walls, David Charlson, Jesse Eline, Tim Kopania, Greg and Shelly Dawson, and Jesse Hamilton. My interns: Antje Jordan, Tim Weber, Marianne Fryer, Honey Storlie and the Heaven in Business track students in Bethel's School of Supernatural Ministry.

THIS BOOK IS DEDICATED TO MY DAD

To quote one of my heroes:
(Rodney Copperbottom from the kids movie Robots)

"Dad, I know you kind of felt bad
when I was growing up
that you couldn't give me a lot of stuff.
But you gave me the most important thing...
You believed in me."

Thanks Dad for modeling and infecting me with this entrepreneurial, pioneering disease that refuses to settle for normal. Thanks for being the greatest champion of me following my heart. Thanks for never drawing back in your relentless pursuit for more of God in every realm of life.

I love you.

INTRODUCTION

What made you pick up this book? I don't know about you, but I am not satisfied with the level of favor, influence and competitive advantage (or lack of it) that the majority of Jesus-followers in the marketplace experience. I have done performance and achieved the results of performance. But there has to be more than just working hard and harvesting the fruits of your labor. Where's God in all this? Is He limited to partnering with people in the pulpit, or is He really interested in the marketplace as well? I believe there has to be more.

I'm now on that journey of experiencing more. I don't believe it ever has to stop. "Of the increase of His government and Peace there is no end" (Isaiah 9:7). I have experienced God's increase personally and have a rapidly growing number of testimonies from all over the world of others experiencing the same. "Christ in you" is the greatest competitive advantage any businessperson could ever hope for. His very Presence is the distinguishing factor that causes you to stand out. It's not compulsory, but it is an invitation. Do you want it?

I have a dream to see one million businesspeople who clearly demonstrate a partnership with God in their place of work—who are distinguished from their colleagues by the tangible Presence of God. The purpose of writing this book is to set you up to experience that partnership. How do you access His wisdom, peace, foreknowledge and increase in your marketplace activities?

How do you realize your dreams without losing your family or friends or health on the way? How do you experience the benefits

---

I have a dream to see one million businesspeople who clearly demonstrate a partnership with
God in their place of work.

---

of having the God of all creation as your partner at work *every* day? Join me on the journey of discovering more.

THE POWER OF TESTIMONY

You will notice that testimonies, or true-life stories, of businesspeople partnering with God are spread throughout this book. Testimonies are the résumé of God. What He has done in the past, He will do again. What He has done for someone else, He can do for you. Testimonies are a key that opens a door for us to go after more. They are the key for us to win (see Revelation 13:12) and prophesy what God will do again (see Revelation 19:10).

I encourage you to make the testimonies personal by remembering them, praying them over your life and then spreading your own testimonies as God shows up on your behalf.

SUCCESS AND THE POWER OF GOD

You *could* read this book and assume that my focus is on what I can get from accessing the limitless supply of a Supernatural God. There is an emphasis on the results, but the method to those results is nothing less than the Person. This message is *not* a get-rich-quick scheme or a shallow assumption that your journey with God will not involve walking through challenges, discomfort or pain. The emphasis on results is to awaken the sleeping body of Jesus-followers who are dormant to the power and purpose they have access to.

Testimonies are the résumé of God.

Success is far more than a profitable balance sheet. It is far more than obtaining provision, protection, power or direction for your business or family. True success involves thriving in *every* area of your life – your heart, mind, and spirit, your marriage, your connection with your children, friends and community. If you succeed in building a multimillion-dollar business, and even transform your city for Christ, but people around you don't experience love, you have failed (see 1 Corinthians 13:1-3). The greatest measure of success is, "Did you learn to love?" God is love and to know God means to know and demonstrate love (see 1 John 4). It is real, it is authentic, it cannot be imitated, it must be experienced.

WHO IS GOD TO YOU?

In beginning this journey to experience more of the Presence and power of God at work, first answer for yourself, "Who is God to me?" You may answer that He is God Almighty, Creator of the Universe, who is to be feared above all else. You may answer that He is the God who associates himself with people—the God of

Abraham, the God of Isaac, the God of Jacob, who redeemed a people from slavery and supernaturally led them into a promised land. You may even answer that He is the God who sent His Son to earth to represent a loving Father and restore face-to-face relationship, as it was in the beginning. This is the God of whom Jesus said, "Go tell My brethren that I am ascending to My Father and your Father, and to My God and your God" (see John 20:17).

In writing this book, I write with an understanding that God is *all* of the above. He is my Creator, He is my Savior, He is my Lord and He is my loving Father who is only good. I invite you into a greater revelation of what it means to be a child of God but at the same time never to forget He is still God.

THE PRESENCE OF GOD

Through this book, you will notice continual reference to the Presence of God. The Presence of God is the very Person of God as experienced by you.

God is everywhere at all times, but we can personally develop our intimacy and awareness of Him with us. In spite of intellectually knowing that God is in us and around us, many of us have never knowingly or intentionally experienced His Presence. That is about to change. Developing an awareness of His Presence with you throughout your daily life is one of the intended outcomes of this book.

For me, the Presence of God is associated with a deep sense of peace. He is the God of all peace and leads us with peace (see Isaiah

9:6, Philippians 4:7). We are to let the peace of God rule in our hearts—to be our internal governor or judge (see Colossians 3:15).

Other common experiences of the Presence of God include a feeling of love (an intrinsic sense of value for who you are) and hope (a positive expectation for the future). We know that God IS love, so it is impossible to know God and not experience love (see 1 John 4:8). Jesus Himself said, "He who has My commandments and keeps them, it is he who loves Me. And he who loves Me will be loved by My Father, and I will love him and manifest Myself to him" (John 14:21).

Whenever people experience the Presence of God, their level of hope for the future increases. I love how Paul prayed, "Now may the God of hope fill you with all joy and peace in believing, that you may abound in hope by the power of the Holy Spirit" (Romans 15:13).

People also experience His Presence in many other ways. I encourage you to develop your own awareness of God's Presence with you. Psalm 46:10 gives us a clue to do this: "Be still and know God." This means to cease from your activities, be quiet, relax and intimately experience God. Thanking Him for His goodness towards you is another simple way of focusing your heart and attention on Him. Then sit quietly and invite Him to make Himself known to you. Be aware of what you experience in your emotions, your thoughts, your spirit and even in your physical body as you develop a consciousness of His Presence, the very Person of God with you.

THE POWER OF AGREEMENT

Jesus said that when two agree on earth concerning anything they ask, it would be done for them by our Father in Heaven (see Matthew 18:19). There is power in agreement.

As you start this book I encourage you to agree with me right now that a never-ending increase in partnership with the Person of God will become your daily experience. I pray that as you journey through these pages, you will be launched into a fresh revelation of how good our Father is. May He be the distinguishing feature that causes your life to literally stand out from all the peoples on the face of the earth (Exodus 33:16). May history record that you were a friend of God.

NOTE FROM THE AUTHOR
The Source of Success

"Without Him I can do nothing."

Jesus

Some people may read this book and focus on the results only—what I call "prostituting the Voice." It's like the individual who was given a goose that laid golden eggs. For the first few weeks, he was delighted in the goose and the golden eggs it produced. But then his greed manifested, and he demanded more and more eggs from the goose. Eventually he killed and cut open the goose to try and get at more eggs. He ended up with nothing. The benefits of God's Presence are far more valuable than a golden egg. But if I allow the outcome to become more important than the Source, then I lose both the Source and the outcome.

If I allow the outcome to become more important than the Source, then I lose both the Source and the outcome.

Moses the Prince, agricultural businessman, Prophet and national leader stood on top of Mt Sinai and said to God, "I would rather die in this stinking hot desert *with* You than get your benefits *without You*." He turned down the protection, provision, direction and power that came with an angel (see Exodus 33:2, 15). He wanted nothing without the Person of God manifested in Peace and Rest—even in a desert. He got what he really desired. He talked face to face with God like a man speaks with his friend. He was known as a friend of God.

In July 2008, we asked God if our future was in the small town where we lived on the East Coast of New Zealand. His answer resulted in our family of six travelling across the world to relocate to Redding, California. We then received specific prophetic words that we were here for "an extended period of time" and that "our Green Card would be easy." Almost four years later (May 2012), we won the Diversity Visa lottery that gave us fast access to an American Green Card (this gives a foreign citizen the same rights of an American, except for voting). Ten months later, we successfully completed the final part of that process, which involved an interview at our local consulate. Approved. God was right after all! We then waited a few weeks for the physical documentation that confirmed what had already transacted.

That process got me reflecting over our journey—this crazy but wonderful adventure with God. We left everything but gained so much. Our fears were exposed, but our trust was built. Our dreams were tested, but our hope was realized. We lost comfort and certainty but found within us more than we could have imagined. We authored a book that has been translated into multiple formats and languages. We developed a DVD curriculum that is being used in schools, churches and community centers in multiple nations. Our story has catalyzed families, businesses, missions, community centers and more. We thought we would give our lives to build the lives of people, but we are now building an *organization* to build the lives of people. How did we stumble on such increase? What was the key to this "success"?

The more I reflect on this, the more I realize the answer is simple. One thing is the secret source of success, now and ongoing. For me, this is best illustrated in the image from the children's animated movie *Megamind*. Minion, an alien fish, is the sidekick of the main character of the movie. Outside of his water-filled space suit, he just flaps around. But in his suit he has the appearance and impact of a super-being! Selah (pause and think deeply on this).

The Presence, the very Person of God, is my water and my space suit. With Him clothing me, I can do *anything*, and I have absolute peace. If I neglect the priority of being filled and clothed with Him, then I freak out and flap around (just ask my wife and kids). He

---

He is the secret source to all success.

---

is the secret source to all success. He is the source of all favor and increase. The closer and more aware of Him I become, the more outstanding "performance" I seem to walk into. However, like Samson and Hezekiah, Gideon and Solomon, and all the heroes of old, the source is not of myself or my hair or my wisdom. The source is Christ.

What is the source of your success? What are you doing to protect and prioritize the Source over the success? What are you doing to keep the main thing the main thing?

NOT WITHOUT YOUR PRESENCE, NOT WITHOUT THE WORLD

Once you have made the Person of God your priority, settle for nothing less than the fullness of what He paid for: life without limits, life more abundantly. Anything that takes away from abundant life becomes your enemy and your mission to destroy— all systems of evil, poverty, disease, slavery and lack.

You have been given Mission Impossible; Will you receive it?

You were not called to be average; you were called to the impossible. You have been given Mission Impossible; will you receive it?

"Spirit lead me where my trust is without borders
Let me walk upon the waters wherever you would call me
Take me deeper than my feet could ever wander
And my faith will be made stronger
In the Presence of my Savior"

"Oceans" by Hillsong United

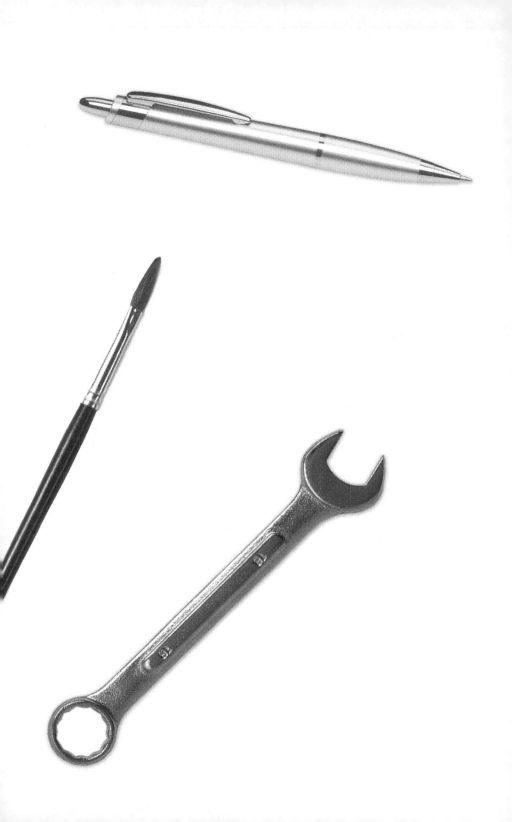

1

The Invitation

"Most assuredly, I say to you, he who believes in Me,
the works that I do he will do also; and greater works than
these he will do, because I go to My Father."

Jesus (see John 14:12)

David was three months into his job as a salesman of crushed walnut shells. One morning during his personal prayer time, he had a very strong impression that God was about to do something significant in his workplace. As he drove the 20 minutes to work, the Presence of God (a tangible peace) in his vehicle became stronger and stronger, along with a deep sense of partnership with Him at work.

Overwhelmed by God, David marched up to his new boss and boldly told him, "God is about to do something at our workplace that no man could do. It will be such a big and amazing thing that no man will be able to take credit for it." His boss was not a follower of Jesus and was shocked (David had never been this bold before).

David then asked, "So what are your dreams for this workplace?" His boss politely replied, "I will let you know if I think of anything."

David walked from the office and suddenly realized what he had just done. "What were you thinking? You have only been here three months, and your boss is going to think you are crazy!" What had seemed perfectly logical moments earlier now seemed foolish to his natural mind.

Three days later David was referred to the CEO of a local Humane Society, who said, "We have discovered a new use for your nutshells, and you need to come and see."

David arrived at the Humane Society and was ushered into two rooms with 25–40 cats in each. Employees began to shove cat litter boxes in his face, telling him: "Smell it." Reluctantly he did and was surprised to find there was no smell. The employees had replaced the standard kitty litter with crushed walnut shells. The CEO of the Humane Society suggested David create and market this as a new product and that he would be willing to help in any way.

Two days later David presented a rough business plan to his boss. The financials showed a margin *seven times* more profitable than any other product in the company's 12-year history. Once his boss was convinced of the potential of this idea, David was called on regularly as a critical link in transitioning the focus of the company. One morning, God even inspired David with the new product's name.

Internally David struggled in this new leadership role over projects he had no prior qualification or experience in. He was now resolving conflicts within the company, producing commercials for TV, making million-dollar decisions on packaging equipment, and was part of decision-making conference calls with the CEO and senior management. In spite of initially being overwhelmed, he started getting words of wisdom from God at key moments that only made him stand out even more (not always to the enjoyment of fellow employees or overlooked managers).

In just nine months from the first time God spoke about doing something significant, the new product was being distributed in all 50 states of the USA and in 12 other nations. At one point his boss acknowledged, "There is something to this prayer thing."

One Friday shortly thereafter, David was called into his boss's office. The company had been sold for millions of dollars, and he was no longer needed. In the midst of the shock, he was escorted off the property.

David was now in the fight of his life not to let offense and bitterness overtake him. How could his boss do this after all David's connections, ideas and hard work had made him a rich man? How could God allow this to happen?

In the midst of this inner battle, another startup company in the same industry contacted David. He had met them a month earlier at a tradeshow. They were developing a new cat litter and wanted him to help test and develop it. On testing it, David was astounded to discover it eliminated odor *ten times* better than any litter he had tested up to that time. Not only that, but it had a profit margin *ten times* that of the previous company's product!

David was then offered the job as the vice president of north American sales. Within three months, he had preorders that exceeded twelve months of sales with the previous company. Far more than being a blessing to this new company, David had discovered an ancient secret: an invitation to partner with God at work.

TEN TIMES GREATER

Daniel was a prophet in history mostly known from children's stories for his adventure in a lion's den. More importantly, in spite of the facts that his nation was defeated, his parents were killed, he was taken captive in a foreign land, and he had to learn a completely new language and culture, Daniel rapidly grew to be one of the most powerful influencers in the global superpower of his day.

If we compared that to today, it would be like a political prisoner of war becoming the President's chief advisor—and he was only in his early 20s at best. How likely is that?

After receiving just three years of language, culture and governance training in this new country, Daniel and his three fellow captives were brought before the king for examination. When King Nebuchadnezzar interviewed them, he found them to be ten times better in wisdom and understanding than all the magicians and astrologers in his entire realm (see Daniel 1:20).

What does ten times greater look like?

What does ten times greater look like? Daniel and his friends were compared to all the advisors and counselors in the entire realm of Babylon. That would be like taking all the wisest people in the world, putting them up against each other and finding four young adults that left the rest looking like they were incompetent.

When is one individual ten times better than the rest, let alone four who have only just learned the language? When has there been a Fortune 500 business that is ten times better than the rest of the highest-ranking companies? We could probably think of some that are one or two times greater, but beyond that, we are left imagining.

So how did Daniel and his friends get so smart? Was their education or training different from that of anyone else? Were they more disciplined, or did they work longer hours? Was it because they had a daily prayer meeting or that they ate vegetarian?

If it were just one person, we would say they were like Einstein—a freak of nature who was a genius from birth and unrivalled during his day. But even with Einstein, was he ten times smarter than his colleagues? I think not; and in the story of Daniel, there were four of them who were ten times greater.

Obviously this was no coincidence!

What was their secret?

What if we could capture that secret and make it a reality in our day?

THE GREATEST MAN ON EARTH

If we skip forward a thousand years or so, we come to another prophet with great influence. His name was John. He dressed somewhat unusually for his day and wandered around in the desert. People came to him from all over Judea and Jerusalem. Even the king of Israel feared him. John preached that people should be baptized to show they had repented of their sins and turned to God to be forgiven (see Mark 1).

Even Jesus submitted to John's teaching and was Himself baptized. There was something about John that moved people to respond, in spite of his appearance and chosen location. If his business was to preach repentance and prepare the way for Jesus, surely it would have been a better business strategy to go where the people were rather than into the desert, making it harder for customers to be served. How did this unusual character attract all of Jerusalem, Judea and the region around the Jordan (see Mathew 3:5) without Facebook, Twitter or some Internet marketing campaign?

Perhaps the answer can be found in this phenomenal statement Jesus made about John:

"Assuredly, I say to you, among those born of women there has not risen one greater than John the Baptist; but he who is least in the kingdom of Heaven is greater than he."

Matthew 11:11

So who was greater, Daniel or John? Who had the greater kingdom influence? According to Jesus, John had greater influence than Daniel. So, if Daniel was ten times better in wisdom and understanding than his peers, what was John?

And just as you are considering the answer to that question, let's consider the One who brought the Kingdom: Jesus.

BRINGING THE KINGDOM

Jesus said that there had not risen one greater than John—up until the point of entry of the kingdom of Heaven. The least in the kingdom of Heaven would be greater than John, and it was Jesus Himself who brought the kingdom of Heaven to earth. Clearly Jesus had greater influence!

Jesus was the fulfillment of centuries-old prophecies. He healed the sick, cleansed lepers, cast out demons and raised the dead. He confounded the rich, the wise and the religious and empowered the poor, the orphans, the women, the children and the slaves. He established the greatest cultural revolution in history, which is still increasing throughout the world today.

37

Jesus also did phenomenal signs and wonders. He turned water into wine, multiplied resources, obtained gold from the mouth of a fish and demonstrated power over the natural elements. What would you do for that kind of power in your business? Think of the profitability of a restaurant that feeds 5,000+ people with a handful of ingredients—and has a full pantry at the end! What if you were a commercial fisherman and you harvested fish and gold coins at the same time, but without needing a fish finder? How about a water bottling company that miraculously became a boutique, high-end winery, but without grapes? What if your business were calming storms or bringing rain that ended drought?

Jesus also had a profound effect on the people He interacted with. He transformed corrupt officials into generous benefactors (see Zaccheus), healed the crippled and insane (see the woman with the issue of blood, the man by pool of Siloam and the wild man of the Gadarenes), gave detailed insight into people's lives (see the woman at the well) and predicted His future with precision.

You will do greater things.

And then, having completely demonstrated what one person can do fully clothed with the Presence and Power of God, this phenomenal Son of God and Son of man declares, *"You* will do greater things" (see John 14:12).

YOU DO GREATER THINGS

I don't know about you, but I am certainly not experiencing the 'ten times better' that Daniel lived in, let alone doing greater works than Jesus! I find it hard to imagine what that would even look like.

Yet if Jesus declared it, then why are we not living it?

Is it possible we have been focusing on doing the ministry of John the Baptist—to preach salvation and point towards Jesus—rather than the ministry of Jesus? Jesus' ministry was to bring the Kingdom of Heaven to every realm of earth He touched.

Is it possible we have been satisfied with kingdom principles but ignored kingdom power?

Is it possible we have been satisfied with kingdom principles but ignored kingdom power?

Is it possible that there is an amazing invitation to "more" than any of us have accessed to this point in our lives?

How hungry are you for more? Are you prepared to pay the price to experience 10 times better, maybe even 1,000 times better than what you are experiencing right now?

What are the keys to stepping into ten times greater than our current standard, let alone greater things than Jesus? What was it that Daniel and his three friends and John the Baptist knew that we don't? Was it some secret principle or commandment? Was it more prayer meetings and less meat in our diet? Was it wearing unusual clothing and hanging out in remote locations? Did they memorize more scripture and spend more frequent time in prayer and fasting? Did they just work harder at it than we do? What was their secret source to success?

THE SECRET TO MORE

I am convinced the secret source to everything they did was the level of connection they had with the very Person of God. They lived as friends of God and accessed the resources of the Limitless One. What we saw was just an overflow of their connection with the Father. They were no different than you or me in their natural ability.

The secret source to everything they did was the level of connection they had with the very Person of God.

Even Jesus said, "Of myself I can do nothing" (John 5:30). That statement is staggering considering He was with God in the beginning and that the worlds were created through Him (see John 1 and Colossians 1:16). But He limited His God-ness to live and die as a human to demonstrate our full potential and serve as an invitation to walk as a child of God just as He did.

Jesus walked in such intimacy and connection with the Father that He could say, "If you have seen Me you have seen the Father" (see John 14:9). Everything He did, He did as a human completely dependent on the Father to come through for Him. As Bill Johnson says; "When we discover that Jesus did great miracles as a man we become completely dissatisfied with our own lives until we see the same."

The cornerstone to living as Jesus did is the revelation that we are His beloved children and then learning to live from a place of intimate fellowship with the Father. His Presence, the very Person of God, becomes our priority—our closest companion and inner compass.

SUMMARY *The Invitation*

- We have an invitation to partner with God in all things, including our daily work.

- Daniel and his three friends partnered with God as advisors to King Nebuchadnezzar. Their wisdom was ten times greater than any of their contemporaries.

- Jesus said John the Baptist was greater than Daniel.

- Jesus set a new standard for what it is for us to partner with God at work (in life).

- Jesus said you would do even greater things than He.

- If Daniel was ten times greater, Jesus was greater than Daniel, and Jesus said you would do greater things than He, what does that say of what is available to you?

- The key to accessing more of God with you at work is your pursuit of intimacy and connection with Him.

- You are invited into friendship with the very Person of God.

- A lifestyle of seeing the Presence and Power of God at work is simply an overflow of personal connection with the Father.

APPLICATION *The Invitation*

1. Meditate on Psalm 8 and take some time to thank Jesus for this incredible invitation to be His friend.

2. Formally invite Jesus into your place of work and your daily activities. Record this moment for future reference.

3. Ask Jesus to show you His ways in your role at work. Set aside time to hear His thoughts and ideas. What is one thing you can do differently this week to involve Him more in your daily activities? What would He love to do? His counsel comes from His friendship with you.

4. Record your daily developments of partnering with God at work. This will be your history of learning to partner with God. It is priceless for reminding yourself and inspiring and equipping others to do the same. For example, you may record, "Asked God this morning for ideas how to move forward with our business expansion. Heard nothing, but this afternoon I literally bumped into a woman at the gas station who turns out to be the perfect solution. Wow! God is with me."

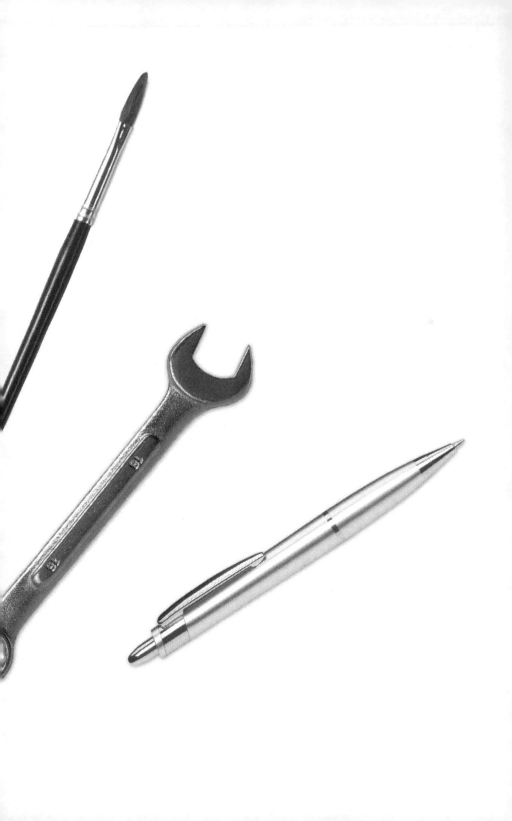

The Performance of Rest

"My Presence will go with you
and I will give you rest."

God (see Exodus 33:13)

Brent was the general manager of a manufacturing company. In spite of only being in his early 30s, he was responsible for over 250 employees and was generating $3 million per month of gross sales.

During the second day of a Heaven in Business workshop, he received word that he was $87,000 below the budgeted net profit of $300,000 for the month (almost 30 percent)!

Normally he would stop everything he was doing and completely focus on doing whatever was necessary to achieve or exceed the budget targets. However, in exploring a partnership with God at work, he chose to lean into what his senior partner could do.

Brent switched off his phone and walked into the event. He focused on resting with God rather than the problem at hand. At the end of the afternoon session titled "The Performance of Rest," Brent turned his phone back on and found two texts and one email.

The first text reported the company had an over-accrual of labor for the previous month, and $40,000 was being credited back to the current month.

The second text reported that an employee, budgeted to cost another $20,000 on sick leave, had suddenly turned back up at work, fully functioning, to the surprise of the management.

Brent then opened the email. It detailed an idea that came from an employee on the manufacturing shop floor. His idea would result in completing a job four weeks ahead of schedule and contribute an additional $35,000 to the month's income!

Within a few hours, a 30 percent deficit became a surplus. When Brent did the opposite of his instincts and rested with God, he was shocked to find the problem was solved so easily. Even better, Brent was gaining confidence in his partnership with God at work and learning His ways of performing from rest.

YOUR BILLIONAIRE-PHILANTHROPIST BUSINESS PARTNER

God has offered to partner with us in our lives on earth. He is not talking about just turning up on Sundays at your local church; He wants to be *with you* in every aspect of your life. Assuming you spend three hours at your local church on a Sunday, that leaves another 98 percent of your week He still wants to be involved with. "God wants us so badly that He has made the condition as simple as He possibly could: 'Only believe.'" Smith Wigglesworth (Plumber by trade, friend of God by occupation, 1859–1947).

In His offer of partnership, God brings a lot to the table. You get ALL of Him.

In His offer of partnership, God brings a lot to the table. You get ALL of Him. That's like having a billionaire philanthropist super-genius as your devoted and loyal business partner. It's not an equal offer, not even close! What does He get out of it? People throughout history have struggled to believe this is for real. Even King David said:

> **"When I look at the night sky and see the work of your fingers—the moon and the stars you set in place—what are mere mortals that you should think about them, human beings that you should care for them? Yet you made them only a little lower than God and crowned them with glory and honor. You gave them charge of everything you made, putting all things under their authority."**
>
> *Psalm 8:3–6 NLT*

This is a crazy offer from our perspective. Would you offer to unconditionally involve yourself in someone else's life, making all your resources available, knowing they are completely incapable without you? Most people don't believe the offer, so they don't even test it out. Others desperately want to access His resources but try to do it on their own terms. The Holy Spirit lives in every believer but rests on few because few have made Him a place of rest (see Isaiah 66:1). What will you do?

The Holy Spirit lives in every believer but rests on few because few have made Him a place of rest.

So what does God bring to the table? What does a partnership with Him look like?

The standout difference from an ordinary partnership includes peace, rest and access to the impossible (wisdom, power, resources, etc.). In this chapter I want to talk about rest: the performance I get from living from the rest that my Partner provides.

A LIFESTYLE OF PEACE AND REST

Most people think resting in peace is something that is inscribed on your tombstone when you die. Jesus offers something different. His offer is a lifestyle of rest and peace. In fact, his name is Prince of Peace, and He promises that as the God of Peace, He will soon crush Satan under your feet (see Romans 16:20). That is violent peace! His peace eradicates anything opposed to freedom and joy. The devil comes to steal, kill and destroy; Jesus brings life and brings it more abundantly (see John 10:10).

So if Jesus brings rest and peace and the devil brings restlessness, striving and pain, who am I most imitating? Whose resources am I partnering with?

If Jesus brings rest and peace and the devil brings restlessness, striving and pain, who am I most imitating?

If we remember way back in history, God offered that His very Presence go with Moses and that He would give Moses rest (see Exodus 33:14). So what does it mean to perform from rest, and how do I access it?

PERFORMANCE AND IDENTITY

Performance is intimately connected to identity. If I don't know who I am or Whose I am, I will perform in order to obtain identity (value). I can only live from rest if I am secure in my identity of knowing that I am a child of God and that He is my source of increase. Typically, people obtain value or identity by what they do. Notice when you meet someone for the first time, the most common question is, "What do you do?" We judge who people are (identity) based on what they do (or don't do). The harder someone works or the higher ranking the position, the more value society places on the individual. We even establish our salary and pay systems on this basis. In my role as a bank manager, I had performance-based compensation. The more results I achieved, the more I was paid. This is not necessarily bad, but it reinforces an internal, "self-focused" belief that my identity is based on what I do.

49

In a partnership with God, the paradigm is different. I get to work from who I am and Who I am with; the belief is God-focused and my identity is based on who He says I am. I live from identity,

---

In a partnership with God, I get to work from rest, not for rest.

---

not for identity. What I do comes from who I am and Whom I am with. Before I even get out of bed in the morning to start my day's work, I am already loved, accepted, valued and significant because I belong to God.

THE ORIGINAL PARTNERSHIP WITH GOD

Look back in the book of Genesis and check out which came first—morning or evening? (See Genesis 1.) God set in place evening first. What do you do in the evening (especially when electricity had yet to be invented)? Not much! The point is, God's "day" for creation starts with the evening; rest comes first in the day.

Now check out the creation of man on the sixth day (see Genesis 1:24–31). God made us, then declared we were good, then had another evening and morning to bring about the seventh day— when God *rested* from all his work (see Genesis 2:2, 3).

So what was the first full day of the week for man? That's right, it was the seventh day—the day of rest. God's plan was for us to work from rest, live from rest, and start our week with rest and intimate connection with Him. Adam had connection with God and found his identity in that fact before he even had a chance to do anything. When we live from that connection, everything starts to flow with Heaven's backing.

God's plan was for us to work from rest, live from rest, and start our week with rest and intimate connection with Him.

The same identity stamp of approval was applied to Jesus before He even did a single miracle. Prior to any public ministry, the Father shouted from Heaven, "This is my beloved Son, in whom I am well pleased" (see Matthew 3:17).

Everything Jesus did and said was to reinstate that original partnership of man with God. There was nothing we could do on our own effort to reinstate that relationship or make us right with God. We were saved by grace, not of works, lest any of us should boast. Salvation is a gift (see Ephesians 2:8).

For we are His workmanship, created in Christ Jesus
for good works, which God prepared beforehand
that we should walk in them.

Ephesians 2:10 NKJV

So, I rest myself into work. I rest myself into the miraculous. I rest by first knowing who I am—Whose I am—and receiving what He has given me. I then get to work from this place of unshakeable

51

identity. Regardless of what happens when I begin to work, my identity is unchanged: I am a child of God; I am a friend of God; I am in partnership with the Creator of the Universe.

WORKING FROM REST

Maria is a highly focused business consultant learning about rest and work. In particular, she highlighted how it is not *either* work *or* rest but *both* flowing together.

Maria says:

Recently I felt an urge to rearrange my bedroom which doubles as my personal workspace. The bed is now where my workstation was and vice versa. I sat down to work and instantly had an inspired thought (that I know to be from God) saying, "You will now rest where you've been working and work where you've been resting."

Meditating on what that meant, a business idea that had been *resting* in my heart and God's hands for a while started to resurface. I started *working* on the business idea, praying and positioning myself practically with first steps to move forward.

Within a week, I happened to meet two significant contacts. One was the main business leader in my nation, who works in the same business field as my idea.

The second connection happened on a day I woke up with a desire to meet a certain architect I had not seen in eight months. This particular morning I decided I wanted to seek him out and prayed for an opportunity to meet him. An hour later I walked into my regular coffee shop and was surprised to see the same architect I wanted to meet, sitting at a table!

The *work* I've done has been out of the *rest* in God and working *with* Him. He sure does all the heavy lifting! I just focus and position myself for advance.

MY JOURNEY: FROM PERFORMANCE TO REST

My own journey of learning to live from rest has taken decades, and it's not finished! To give some context, I tend towards more of a Type A personality. On the DISC behavioral assessment, I

Is it possible we have been satisfied with kingdom principles but ignored kingdom power?

test at 70 percent Dominance, 100 percent Influence, 70 percent Steadiness and 4 percent Conscientiousness. According to Jason Hedge of DISC-U.org, this means "my performance style is fast paced, active and I'm driven to action in order to influence my environment and those around me." That means I don't naturally find it easy to sit still. Work is fun for me.

Add a religious upbringing to all that, and you get performance on steroids. Religion without relationship drives you to attempt to work for something that is a gift. I had the unconscious belief:

"If I work hard and perform my best, I will succeed, be accepted and feel good about myself."

Initially, my external results reinforced my internal performance-based identity. I left school at 17 and did a two-year cadetship on a large training farm in Hawkes Bay, New Zealand (with 20 farm cadets, some horses and dogs, 12,000 sheep and 500 cattle). During this time, I won the prize for "Top Junior" and then "Top Academic Senior."

I went on to university, where I performed to obtain first class honors in agricultural science, specializing in agricultural business management. During my final year, I won a scholarship that led to employment with New Zealand's leading agricultural consultancy firm at the time.

The consultancy business had what was called a "One Ton Club," which was recognition for consultants who reached a certain amount of net chargeable fees. I hit this by year three, and my boss was super impressed with my performance; I just needed to "do the time" and acquire a few gray hairs for my influence to grow in the industry.

Not satisfied with waiting around for my influence to grow, I changed occupations to become a relationship manager with New Zealand's leading agricultural bank. My job was to manage the needs of a portfolio of agricultural and horticultural business clients. Within three years, the portfolio doubled from $50 million to $100 million as the economy was booming. I was also chosen to be a participant in the Kellogg's Rural Leaders Program that develops emerging agribusiness leaders to help shape the future of New Zealand agribusiness and rural affairs.

On the back of my rising business performance, I was also growing in influence and responsibility in my local church. I was on the board of trustees, led worship, and ran a finance course as well as a men's discipleship group. I was also doing mission work in Uganda, helping develop microfinance and orphan programs, as well as leadership development in a regional network of churches.

If that's not enough, at the time my wife and I had three children under the age of five. I married well!

But then things changed. In spite of believing in faith, doing my best and confidently telling my work colleagues a promise that God had spoken about increased business for the year of 2005, I lost one of my biggest clients—a $2 million deal. The next year, I lost a $4 million client. Even though I continued to get performance bonuses and recognition from the bank, I was starting to wake up in the night anxious about the results.

Then in 2007, I lost my largest client ($6 million portfolio). They were purchasing another property and chose to go with a competing bank. I was shocked. It didn't make sense. This was personal! This client was the training farm on which I had been a cadet. As a consultant for them, I had developed and implemented a government-funded training program that significantly

55

upgraded the previous training. They were my friends! In spite of hearing them say it was just a business decision, it meant more than that to me. I took their decision personally.

My thoughts were going wild. "If God is with me (at least more than He is with others), how can I be losing? How can it be that I am walking in faith and right relationship and working with excellence, yet not performing?"

Cracks were appearing in the foundation of my identity. I was waking up in the night anxious about my performance. Anxiety is evidence of an inferior kingdom. Evidence was being revealed that my identity was based on what I did rather than who I was, or *Whose* I was.

One evening after about three months of this, as I was getting into bed and again complaining to my wife about my performance woes, she said, "You need to sort this out!"

"What do you mean?" I said.

"You need to get with God and sort out why you are taking this so personally," she responded. Apparently she had been saying this to me for the last three months, but I'd only just heard it. So I listened to my wife and went back into the living room to "sort it out" with God.

Initially, I just paced the floor and started to tell God all the things that had happened and how I felt so ripped off. "Where were You when these things happened to me?"

In spite of being a follower of Jesus for over 20 years, I'd just had the heart revelation that God is WITH ME.

The next thing I knew, all this pent-up emotion started to come up from within me and leak out my eye sockets. "What was wrong with me??!!" It was like I was experiencing each of the moments of "loss" again, but this time as I knelt on the floor, I could see the feet of Jesus standing beside me and feel His Presence with me. I suddenly had a revelation that He was with me. He was with me!

This exposed the lie that had been hidden under my anxiety. I believed that God is good and is the source of my success, so if I'm not succeeding or performing, God must not be with me. Wow! That sounds really stupid now, but that's the case with most lies

---

You cannot fully experience that God is with you until you have the opportunity to experience the opposite.

---

that we believe. The truth is God is with me, period. In spite of being a follower of Jesus for over 20 years, I'd just had the heart revelation that God is WITH ME—it even happens to be one of His names (Emmanuel)!

You cannot fully experience that God is with you until you have the opportunity to experience the opposite. You cannot learn to trust God until you have the opportunity *not* to. For you to be *more* than a conqueror (see Romans 8:37), you must have some monumental challenge to overcome. I was coming to terms with this fact that very night!

When I finally got to bed, nothing had changed externally, but I finally had a greater peace inside.

During this time, I was reading John Wooden's book *Wooden on Leadership*. He took a University basketball team to national victory ten times in twelve seasons. Everything changes in twelve seasons—the players, the conditions, even the rules. So what

---

"My value is not based on winning or losing but in knowing I gave my best." - *John Wooden*

John Wooden did was legendary. He understood the principles of performance and success. Yet he made this statement that rocked me: "My value is not based on winning or losing but in knowing I gave my best."

I had been basing my value from my winning or losing. I was now having a revelation about my identity. My significance, satisfaction and security—my identity and value—come from being with Father God. It is His Presence with me that gives me value.

So do I not care about losing a client or something that doesn't go to plan? No way! I give my best, period. I expect increase (see Isaiah 9:7), I expect the miraculous (see Mark 16:17). But I am unmoved. My value is not based on the external results but on my internal connection with my Father, God. As King David said (paraphrased from Psalm 16:8):

"I have made my resolve to set my heart continually on Heaven; because I am continually aware of Your Presence, I WILL NOT BE MOVED."

My internal shift was so significant that people around me noticed. Within two months, a brand-new role came up at the bank: a regional new business manager. The role involved travelling and leading the region in training and acquiring new business. Would you have promoted the individual in the branch who had lost the

---

No longer was my identity based on the outcome; my identity and value were based on the fact that God was WITH ME.

---

most business? Probably not. Yet, God has a sense of humor—I was given the new role! Not only that, but in between accepting the role and actually starting the new position, a $10 million deal basically walked into my office. Did I look good or what?!

But no longer was my identity based on the outcome; my identity and value were based on the fact that God was WITH ME.

When I live from that identity, knowing I am His and He holds me and that I get to live *from* rest, then literally nothing is impossible!

I am still on a journey of learning to live from rest, but the life I now live is well beyond what I previously experienced. The favor, connections and influence astound me. My expectations for the future continue to increase exponentially compared to what I could have imagined five years ago. But in all the highs and lows of the journey, I'm learning again and again that my significance, my Source and my satisfaction are found in His Presence. When I live from that identity—knowing I am His and He holds me and that I get to live *from* rest—then literally nothing is impossible!

SUMMARY *The Performance of Rest*

- God has offered to partner with us in our entire life on earth. Life is way more than a Sunday church service.

- The Holy Spirit lives in every believer but rests on few because few have made Him a place of rest.

- Most people think resting in peace is something inscribed on your tombstone; Jesus offers a lifestyle of peace and rest.

- Performance is intimately connected to identity.

- If you don't know who you are or Whose you are, you will perform in order to obtain identity.

- You can only live from rest if you are secure in your identity of knowing that you are a child of God and that He is your source of increase.

- In partnership with God, I get to work from rest, not for rest. I live from identity, not for identity. What I do comes from who I am and Who I am with.

- Jesus restored full partnership with God. God's plan was to work from rest, live from rest and start our week with rest— intimate connection with Him. When we live from that perspective, everything starts to flow with Heaven's backing.

- Anxiety is evidence of an inferior kingdom; it is an invitation to greater intimacy with God.

APPLICATION *The Performance of Rest*

1. When performance doesn't go as planned or you are restless, how do you respond? Where do you turn for comfort? What does your response tell you about your identity? What does your response tell you about what you trust the most?

2. Ask God what lies you believe about your identity and performance. Offer the lies to Him in exchange for the truth. What truth does He want to say to you about your identity and performance? How much does He want to be involved with you in your business?

3. Anxiety is evidence of an inferior kingdom. What is the Father offering or inviting you into instead of fear and anxiety? Make a plan to be more aware of what you do when you feel anxious. What could you do instead? What will you do instead?

4. Invite God into a greater measure of partnership with you in your daily work life. Make a plan to protect your rest—your awareness of God with you every moment of the day. How could you practically do this? How could you set aside time? How could you remind yourself?

Restoring Sonship—
Living from Inheritance

**My success is not my own;
I live from inheritance.**

In order to accept the invitation to more—of partnering with God at work—we need to fully grasp the position we have been given in Christ. We are no longer orphans, foreigners, aliens, servants or slaves. We have been brought into the family, the inheritance of God. You could never come close to earning the inheritance of God; it is a gift, and it can *only* be received.

The key to receiving your inheritance of God is living from intimacy, connection and a confident dependence on Him. It's about getting really good at asking and receiving—just like a child (see Matthew 18:3). The problem is our orphan mentality tries to earn or perform for something that has been given to us. We therefore sabotage our ability to receive. So, are you still living as an orphaned servant, or are you fully living in the freedom and inheritance of a son or daughter? How would you know?

Brad was a graphic designer in the media department of a medium-sized company. As part of a team exercise, they were each asked what lies they believed that were holding them back from pursuing their dreams. Each team member then gave the lie to Father God and asked Him what the truth was that He wanted to give in exchange. After waiting five minutes, the facilitator asked the group what the lie was and what they received in exchange. Brad announced that the lie he had believed was that he was "not good enough." A number of others in the group confessed to having the same lie. But when Brad announced what he received in exchange, a holy hush came over the whole team. When Brad gave up the lie to God, in exchange he heard the Father say, "I made you; who gave you the right to assess yourself?!"

Orphans grow up without the presence of a father or mother. They do not have the comfort, stability or safe environment that loving parents provide in a home. They do not receive their identity from belonging to a family, so they typically build their identity around some form of accomplishment or accumulation of things. In spite of this, they never feel like they belong and never feel satisfied. Their internal void cannot be filled with external things.

Orphans learn from a very young age that they need to look after themselves, protect themselves and provide for themselves because if they don't, no one else will. They say, "If it's going to be, it's up to me." They don't know what it is for someone to nurture and develop them or help them in realizing their dreams. Because they grow up without the presence of a father or mother, they never learn love, trust or connection. They don't know rest or peace.

As it is in the natural, so it is in the spiritual. We were all orphans because we were separated from the Presence of God our Father. The result of original sin was that Adam and Eve left home. They left the Presence of a loving Father. They set themselves against Fathers love, and the resulting curse was separation and toil. Adam and Eve became orphans. When you remove the presence of a father from any environment, you create an orphan culture. When you remove God (who is love) from any environment, you end up with an orphan culture. Even though we may have reconnected with God as our Heavenly Father, most of us have yet to fully embrace what it means to live as a son or daughter of God.

MY IDENTITY CHALLENGE

In the previous chapter I shared my story of learning to live from rest. Through my three-year process of losing business, I gained a revelation that God was WITH ME. Very shortly after that revelation, I was promoted to being the regional new business manager, and a $10 million deal seemingly jumped into my lap.

However, the day that I was supposed to officially start the new role, I handed in my notice to leave the bank. God spoke to my wife and me about leaving everything and going to a new country—a place we had never been before and where we knew no one. It was just at the point when I thought my community influence and internal condition were perfect for God to use me greatly in my region! What kind of strategic decision is that: just when you have your player in the right condition and position, you pull him off the field?

So with four children under the age of eight, we left everything—family, home, growing favor and influence in church and city—to come to Bethel Church in Redding, California.

If your identity is in position, possessions, connection or influence, then this is the perfect opportunity to have it turned upside down. I became one of 800 students at the school of ministry, hidden in the midst of a multitude. We ended up selling our home to pay for our "adventure." We sold or gave away all our household items in New Zealand and did our best to scrape together the necessary items here, not knowing how long the house fund would need to provide for us. We affectionately called this "eating our house"— something I had said I would never do. By my calculations, the funds would last about three years.

At the end of the first year, I had a divine connection with Danny Silk, who was the family life pastor at the time. I was the perfect solution to what he was wanting to build for the staff of Bethel Church – helping them realize their dreams. I had no idea that the last 15 years of my life had prepared me for this, perfectly! I interned with him, and under his leadership, we built Dream Culture and then Global Transformation Institute.

At the end of the second year, we discussed coming on staff. However, we were starting a new department, and there were budget restrictions at the time, so there would be no new hires. Going into the third year, I just continued what I was doing and called it a second internship.

In the midst of this, I was questioning whether God was providing for me or whether I needed to take matters into my own hands and do something to provide for myself. Where was He? Where was the provision of a God who was WITH ME? Was I wrong to trust God this much? Or maybe there was something wrong with me?

Midway through the third year, I was starting to feel anxious about finances again. The head gasket blew on our vehicle, and our son ended up with a $1,500 dentist bill (this would have been free in New Zealand). We were into the third year of "eating" our house, and we were almost done! At what point was it responsible to end our adventure and return to an income in New Zealand? If we returned, we would still need to start all over again: job, car, basic home setup with four children. What would that cost? This was not fun, and it was definitely not my view of success.

So, to avoid facing that pressure (busyness is another form of denial), I went with Danny on a ministry trip to Alaska. I figured I would be fully occupied with ministry and serving Danny by managing the resource table.

I was wrong. They had volunteers for everything! I was left alone with my financial worries in the midst of a bunch of crazy Alaskans worshipping an awesome God who is always good.

In that moment, I made a decision to hold onto what God had said—His promises, His direction. Regardless of what happened, I would hold on and trust Him. I closed my eyes and lifted my hands in a posture of faith and determination: "God, *I* won't let go of you."

Then I opened my eyes, and a painting caught my eye. During worship, a local artist, Jamie Bottoms, had painted an image of an arm coming down from Heaven gripping onto an arm going up from earth. It was titled "Never Let You Go." Exactly! "God, *I* will never let You go!"

But as I looked closer at the painting, I realized that God's arm was much bigger and His hand much stronger than mine. If any pressure came on that connection, my hand would be the first to let go. Actually, I could completely let go, and it would make no difference at all to His grip.

Imagine a four-year-old walking down an unstable path, holding hands with his father and saying, "Dad, I won't let you go." "Sure, son," the dad replies with a smile. Dad knows that at the first sign of falling, he will lift his son up by his hand.

I realized it wasn't about me holding onto Him but knowing that He had a hold of me. There is nothing I could do to lessen his grip on me. He will never let go of ME! He is WITH ME!

Again, something shifted internally in my understanding of my identity as a child of God.

I trust not in my ability to hold onto Him but in His ability to hold onto me.

It's not about my performance or my ability or even my level of trust; it's about His Nature as Father. He really does have a hold of me. He really does care for me. He really does have good things He wants to give me, but my thinking must change in order to receive. If I receive what He wants to give me while my thinking is on my ability and performance, I am reinforcing an inferior mentality as an orphan or slave. When I have a revelation of how much of a loving Father He is, limitless in grace and goodness and more committed to my wellbeing than I am, I can receive so much more from His hand without it altering my identity as a son.

My anxiety about how God was going to come through for me and my family turned into anticipation about *what* He was going to do. He had a grip on me and would never let go. I could genuinely relax. I had found peace. I had found a new level of resting in Him—in His hand.

Again, nothing changed externally in that moment. But three months later, under Danny's influence and still as an intern, I co-authored and published a book with my wife about partnering with God in the dreams and desires of our hearts. (See next chapter: Dreaming with God.) Twelve months later we were on staff and moving forward. Two years later I continue to grow in my amazement of how good God is as my loving Father. I am beginning to see that we have only scratched the surface of how much more God has in store for us. Everything comes from my connection with Him and my ability to receive like a child.

> **"I tell you the truth, anyone who doesn't receive the Kingdom of God like a child will never enter it."**
>
> *Jesus, Son of God (see Luke 18:17 NLT)*

Where are you on your journey of knowing God as Father and living as a son or daughter? How much of your success is from your own efforts, or is there evidence to demonstrate an intimate connection of a limitless God showering you with favor and increase? Who truly got you to where you are today?

You were not born to start from zero.
You were born to live from inheritance.

SELF-MADE ORPHANS

Think of the most widely known, successful people in business, and most likely you will mention a person who has gone from nothing to millions of dollars of "net worth." Our business culture has exalted the self-made millionaire who has forged their success through unwavering drive, vision and hard work all on their own. The only problem is that *self-made* can be another name for *orphan*. You were not born to start from zero. You were born to live from inheritance.

If you are going to access the increase that comes from God, you can only access it through inheritance.

The predominant business culture reinforces an atmosphere likened to a global orphanage: you have to make it on your own, and we recognize and respect you if you do. It is not so with God. If you are going to access the increase that comes from God, you can only access it through inheritance.

**I have lived to perform and
attained the results of performance;
I want to see the results of Presence.**

ORPHAN CULTURE OR CULTURE OF SONSHIP

Evidence of an orphan culture is easy to identify in the corporate business environment. It is commonly filled with dishonor and disempowerment to the point that when you start to succeed, another orphan will cut you down or shut you out. It is fueled by a win-lose or scarcity mentality: "If you win, then I will lose (or become less)." Ultimately it is fueled by fear: "I am afraid I will lose my portion or position, so I will do anything to protect myself.

I worked really hard to get to this position, so I'm not going to let you walk on past me without a fight. I had to fight to get this success, so you are going to have to do the same if you want it."

Not so with God. If we are going to access His inheritance, we can only do it His way. His only fuel and motivation is love. His increase is a gift, not a payment for performance. If we want to access the increase that comes from inheritance, we have to live as sons and daughters. If we want a business that accesses Heaven's supply, we must set it up on Heaven's values, Heaven's culture. Heaven's culture is a culture of Sonship.

If we want a business that accesses Heaven's supply, we must set it up on Heaven's values.

Danny was working for a foster care agency that was at the same time paying for him to work towards his master's degree in social work. The owner was like a father to Danny and was developing him to take over the company. Shortly after completing his master's degree, Danny was asked by another mentor in his life to be part of the leadership staff of a non-profit organization. Danny was now torn between his loyalty to his foster care "father" and this new opportunity to step into what he felt was the next step in following the call of God in his life.

After wrestling with the decision, he went to the owner of the foster care agency and told him about the opportunity and his struggle in making a decision. The owner promptly said, "If there is *anything* that I have done to contribute to your success, then I count it a privilege." Danny was forever impacted by this heart-wrenching experience of a culture of Sonship.

If there is *anything* that I have done to contribute to your success, then I count it a privilege.

Evidence of a culture of Sonship includes encouraging and empowering (giving power to) people around you; you become a catalyst rather than a container. In a culture of Sonship, value is placed on connection, and people are valued for who they are *more* than for what they can do. Accordingly, honor is demonstrated by holding people accountable to the fullness of their capabilities as a person, not just as an employee—they are equipped with tools to discover the dreams and potential within and given opportunity and support to live from purpose. As a result, creativity and risk-taking are encouraged, and the environment is continually expanding, just like a healthy family.

THE ORPHAN CYCLE

The following diagram represents the orphan cycle in business. The foundation is disconnection—from those above you, those around you and those that follow. Starting with an orphan or slave mentality, you only experience increase from what you fight or strive for—"earn it!" As a result you live for what you can get rather than what you can give. You limit others from going further by making them start off where you started off: zero. If they are talented, they will get to where you are…maybe.

Your significance, satisfaction and success come from your performance and independence, protected from what others may or may not do.

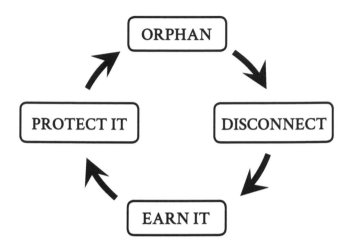

In an orphan culture, we ultimately get a boom/bust cycle. One generation fights from the dust to realize a measure of success. The orphan mentality then holds on to protect the success and keep all others at a distance unless they can build something from zero in their own right. The following generation sees the separation and protection and price paid and is then either satisfied to live as a slave under the control of the orphan leader or goes elsewhere to start from zero. This is why so many businesses fail when the second and third generation family members take over.

THE CYCLE OF SONSHIP

The contrast is the cycle of Sonship (or family) shown in the next diagram. The foundation is connection. Heaven starts and ends with family. How well are we representing that in our lives?

"Any time we leave connection or the concept of family, we leave the concept of kingdom."

Bill Johnson

The Kingdom of God does not differentiate between sector of society, occupation or economic status. If we are part of His Kingdom, it affects *every* aspect of life to the same measure and is forever increasing in influence (see Isaiah 9:7).

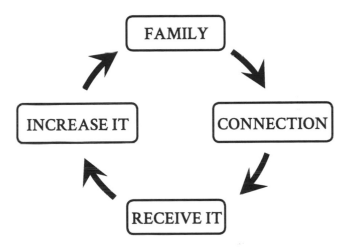

In the cycle of Sonship, we establish a momentum of perpetual increase. From the foundation of connection, we set up inheritance, legacy or an inherent environment where people step into the existing success they did nothing to work for—they received it purely by being part of the "family." Success is no longer my independence or ability to protect what I have. It is now seeing others access my momentum and go further: those around me go beyond me. I set up a legacy so that generations yet to be born are better off because of my influence.

The Kingdom of God does not differentiate between sector of society, occupation or economic status. If we are part of His Kingdom, it affects *every* aspect of life.

SONSHIP AND ENTITLEMENT

What happens when you take an orphan into a palace, but the orphan never changes his or her outlook on life? Orphans will take advantage of the environment without embracing the responsibility to contribute to its advancement. This is called entitlement.

Entitlement turns a gift into a demand or "right." It is ignorant of or belittles the sacrifice and price paid by previous generations that purchased the current levels of freedom and empowerment. Entitlement blinds sons and daughters to the responsibility that comes with inheritance.

Success is no longer my independence or ability to protect what I have. It is now seeing others access my momentum and go further; those around me go beyond me.

Entitlement is evidence of an orphan heart. It will undermine inheritance and sabotage the cycle of momentum, passing on debt rather than greater measures of empowerment. Unchecked, entitlement will turn a nation of sons and daughters into a nation of orphans and slaves.

Sonship does the opposite; it recognizes and values the price paid and seeks to honor those who invested their lives by going further, faster, stronger and longer. Sons and daughters seek to access the fullness of the price that was paid and appropriate that in even greater levels in generations yet to come. In doing so, sons and daughters become fathers and mothers.

Unchecked, entitlement will turn a nation of sons and daughters into a nation of orphans and slaves.

The quickest ways to kill entitlement are to regularly acknowledge what others have contributed to your current levels of success and always seek to increase this for others around you. How have you recently demonstrated appreciation for those who paid a price for you to experience what you are experiencing? Ask yourself what you are doing with the favor and privilege that you have. How are you growing it and releasing it as momentum for others?

SONSHIP, MERCY AND GRACE

By mercy you don't get what you deserve.
By grace you get what you don't deserve.
Mercy restores you to zero;
grace takes you to infinity and beyond!

Sonship requires an understanding of grace. Grace is far more than mercy. Through mercy you *didn't* get what you deserved. You deserved punishment for your wrongdoing, but you obtained forgiveness or release from your debt. Heaven visited you and wiped your slate clean.

Mercy gets you to zero, but grace is a release of momentum that takes you to infinity and beyond! Through grace you get what you don't deserve. By grace we are made alive again, raised up to the original position of authority and power, and re-established in the fullness of what God intended for our lives—good works that he prepared In advance that we should walk in them.

Jesus did not come for you to simply live free and die in peace. He came for you to live in Presence and Power, just like He demonstrated—and greater things.

Mercy gets you a visit from the King. But by grace you get invited to live with the King and eat continually at His table—*with* Him! By grace you get to access everything that is in the King's house and storeroom. You cannot earn it; that would be works. You just have to receive it like a child.

"But God, who is rich in mercy,

because of His great love with which He loved us,

even when we were dead in trespasses,

made us alive together with Christ

(by grace you have been saved),

and raised [us] up together,

and made [us] sit together

in the heavenly [places] in Christ Jesus,

that in the ages to come He might show

the exceeding riches of His grace

in [His] kindness toward us in Christ Jesus.

For by grace you have been saved through faith,

and that not of yourselves; [it is] the gift of God,

not of works, lest anyone should boast.

For we are His workmanship,

created in Christ Jesus for good works,

which God prepared beforehand

that we should walk in them."

Ephesians 2:4–10

SUMMARY *Restoring Sonship*

- We have been brought into the family, the inheritance of God. This cannot be earned; it is a gift, and it can only be received.

- An orphan mentality tries to earn or perform for what is a gift and therefore sabotages your ability to receive.

- If you are going to access the increase that comes from God, you can only access it through inheritance.

- An orphan culture is fueled by fear, founded on disconnection, and filled with dishonor and disempowerment. It results in a boom/bust cycle.

- A culture of Sonship (family and inheritance) is fueled by love, founded on connection and filled with honor and empowerment. It results in a momentum of perpetual increase.

- Entitlement is evidence of an orphan heart. It turns a gift into a demand or "right."

- Sonship recognizes, values and celebrates the contribution and success of others.

- Sonship requires an understanding of grace—where people are trusted and promoted beyond what they deserve (or "earn").

- We need to learn to receive—like a child.

APPLICATION *Restoring Sonship*

1. How free are you? Mark each of the following on a continuum of where you see yourself. For example, do you live with God as your master or more as your Abba Father? Is your primary motivation obedience or love? Do you live with the revelation that He holds you, completely? Where are you on this scale?

ORPHANS   SONS

God is boss ------------------------------------ God is Father

Told what to do ----------------------------- Asked what to do

Fear, obedience ---------------------------------- Love, desire

Live for connection ----------------------- Live from connection

Restricted access ------------------------------------ Full access

Have to hold on ----------------------- Know you are held onto

Payment -- Inheritance

Protect -- Trust

Earn, perform -------------------------------------- Receive

Compare -------------------------------------- Celebrate others

Doing -- Being

2. Take some time to set your mind on things above and experience the love of the Father towards you. Ask Him what lies you have believed about your identity as His son or daughter. Offer the lie up to Him and ask Him to take it away.

3. Now ask the Father who He says you are. What does He want to give you in exchange for the lies you gave up to Him? (He always gives good things.) What do you need to believe about yourself in order to fully live as a son or daughter of God?

4. What is one thing you will do this week to partner with who the Father says you are? How will you live as a son or daughter?

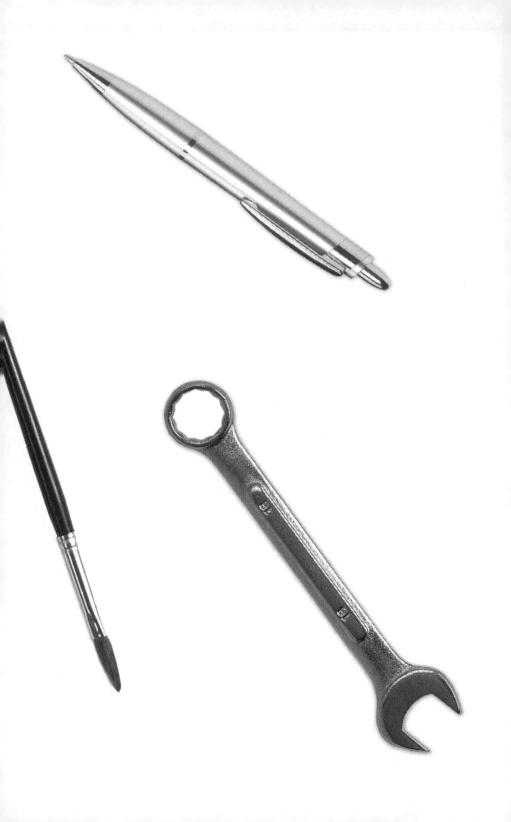

Dreaming with God

"Beware lest anyone cheat you
through philosophy and empty deceit,
according to the tradition of men,
according to the basic principles of the world,
and not according to Christ."

Colossians 2:8 (emphasis added)

Peter was a successful graphic designer with over ten years of experience in his industry, but he had always dreamed of becoming a full-time wildlife artist. Living in Durban, South Africa, there was limited access to training in fine art painting techniques and not many art galleries to even display the art. On top of that, only the best artists could make a living from their trade, so Peter was advised by friends and family to stay with his graphic design business. Why would he leave a well-paying, steady business to start from zero in an unpredictable and uncertain industry?

But Peter had a competitive advantage—"Christ inside." As he says, "Dreamers are born to demonstrate the impossible." So in partnership with the Holy Spirit, Peter launched out after his dream regardless of the opposition. Daily he would pray and ask for supernatural help as he explored different painting techniques and rapidly grew in the skills to perform his craft at a high standard.

Dreamers are born to demonstrate the impossible.

He was told by other international artists that he would never get into this gallery, as he had to "pay his dues," which would take years of hard work and study. However, within just six months of full-time painting, he was invited to exhibit in one of America's top wildlife art galleries in Florida!

As Peter says, "Holy Spirit, you are awesome and the best teacher and guide I could ever have!"

A COMPETITIVE ADVANTAGE

What is the competitive advantage of being a follower of Christ in business? Is it not Christ inside? (See Colossians 1:27.) But what does "Christ in me" really mean? Is that just a set of principles, kingdom business principles?

As a businessperson building a successful enterprise, how would you feel if you found out someone was defrauding you of hundreds of thousands, if not millions of dollars? What if they were keeping you from the true potential of a business idea or withholding favor and connections? "But I follow Christ, that couldn't happen to me." Not so. I believe the majority of Christ-followers are being defrauded or cheated out of a great deal of abundant living because they are not tapping into the full potential of Christ in us. Here's how the Apostle Paul wrote it:

> **"Beware lest anyone *cheat you* through philosophy**
> **and empty deceit, according to the tradition of men,**
> **according to *the basic principles* of the world,**
> **and not according to *Christ*."**
>
> *Colossians 2:8 (emphasis added)*

So are the basic principles of the world bad? Not necessarily. In this case, the writer was referring to self-imposed sacrifice and benevolent actions (religion), the appearance of servant leadership (humility) and the determined discipline of self in order to succeed (see Colossians 2:23). We could also include principles like hard work, initiative, cooperation, loyalty and so on. You can obtain a measure of success in life with them—look at any highly successful businessperson, and you can quickly identify them. But according to God's standard of abundant living, on their own they will leave you short-changed. The key, the true substance, is Christ—God in man—absolute power governed by absolute love.

PARTNERSHIP WITH A LIMITLESS GOD

Christ demonstrated what a human could do in complete partnership with a limitless God. The partnership He demonstrated was not a business contract or an agreement for exchange of services. It wasn't a set of commandments or principles to live by. It was personal; it was a covenant relationship.

Christ demonstrated what a human could do in complete partnership with a limitless God.

That means Jesus gave all of Himself, and God gave all of Himself. Heart, mind, soul, body. "Everything I have is yours." Any time we reduce our covenant with God to a set of rules, we miss the whole point of why Christ came to earth and rob ourselves of abundant life.

When you have fully yielded your life to Christ, you get ALL of Him. "It pleased the Father that in Him the fullness would dwell" (see Colossians 1:19). What does the fullness of God demonstrated in human form look like? It looks like Christ:

Water to wine
Gold in a fish's mouth
Multiplication of resources
Power over natural elements
Fish where there were no fish
Power over sickness and evil spirits
Wisdom and poise that completely foiled his opposition
Foreknowledge of assassination (or hostile takeover) attempts
And how about walking on water or even walking through a wall!

Go back over this list and think of what the fullness of God could look like in your business. What would you give to have a medical

---

Any time we reduce our covenant with God to a set of rules, we miss the whole point of why Christ came to earth and rob ourselves of abundant life.

---

facility where people got healed in the waiting room as well as through the surgical process? What if your security and personal protection company knew ahead of time exactly where and when criminal attempts would be made? What if your horticultural company didn't just sell products, but also prayed for dead plants that came back to life? What if your company or department had a workforce with zero annual sick days? What if your food warehouse restocked itself? What if every customer who came into contact with your business left full of hope and peace? What if your construction business was not just known for excellence, but everywhere they built, the surrounding land became more productive? What if?

When you have fully yielded your life to Christ, you get ALL of Him.

Just to clarify, this is not some supernaturally infused self-enrichment program, but the power to fully establish Heaven on earth. It is not about what I can get, but what I can give. The gift of Sonship gives me access to limitless supply in order to establish a Kingdom on earth that fully reproduces Heaven. The ultimate goal is *all creation* fully alive (see Romans 8:18–21).

The ultimate goal is *all creation* fully alive.

As the cofounder of a substance abuse treatment center, **Philip** wrote down a God-dream: "To stand before Congress and give solutions to the social problems our nation is facing."

Two months later, the governor of his state nominated him as "one of the most distinguished citizens of 2012" for his work in the substance abuse field. As a result of this nomination, he was asked to speak to the state legislature about the work they were doing and offer suggestions to maximize success in the non-profit sector. State legislators were genuinely impressed and confounded by the success the program had achieved compared to similar programs.

Three months after speaking to the legislature, he was asked to sit on a state strategic planning team. The team travelled to Baltimore to meet with various members of the legislature, military, joint chiefs, and other members of the federal (national) government. As he sat in the room sharing ideas about how to solve the social problems in the nation, he was overwhelmed with a sense of God's destiny and purpose over his life.

As Philip said, "Honestly, when I wrote that dream, I did not really even have the faith to believe that it was possible. I have since been overwhelmed with the reality that God has really, *really* big plans for us. What an honor to dream with Him!"

Geovany and his family own a manufacturing company that produces high-end stone and ceramic mosaics. They received a large order that required rare slate stone from the Amazon jungle. Acquisition of this stone became very difficult due to governmental restrictions for environmental protection.

The company had previously purchased 50% of the raw materials needed. Francisco (Geovany's brother) sought out how they might acquire the balance. However, after exhausting every option, they were not able to find any alternative sources. Feeling the pressure of only being able to deliver half the order, the family met together to pray and ask God for a solution.

That week, the factory supervisor called: "We have begun to process the stone. Some pieces are breaking because they are thicker than usual. One of the workers tapped a piece of it with his hammer, and it split into two. Other pieces of stone split into three!"

Francisco was astounded. "So, how long would it take to split all the remaining stone?" The supervisor responded, "It's really fast, and it speeds up the rest of the process. We can finish the order within a week and we won't be needing more raw materials."

Not only did they meet the order on time, they did it at half the cost. They even "discovered" a better method to process this type of stone. God with you at work is highly profitable!

YOU HAVE PERMISSION TO DREAM WITH GOD

You also are invited to access the fullness of the covenant partnership you signed up for in making Christ your Lord.

You have permission to access limitless supply—He lives in you! You have permission to dream and partner with the God who formed the world and holds the universe together. You have permission to create, design, explore and discover. You are His son or daughter. He loves you and is proud of you because you belong to Him.

You have permission to dream.

You have permission to succeed.

You have permission to demonstrate how good God really is— how much of an extravagantly loving Father He is. The world is waiting. All creation is waiting! (See Romans 8:19.)

THE WORLD IS WAITING FOR YOU

"The single greatest vacuum in the world today is the knowledge of the nature of God as Father."

Bill Johnson

God's nature as Father is not revealed by merely meeting your needs; even a prison warden will provide you with a bed, a blanket and basic food. The nature of God as Father is revealed in meeting your desires: the dreams of your heart. When we live from our heart—from the dreams and desires within us—life is released (see Proverbs 13:12), our joy is made manifest and we show the world how good our Father God is. We *must* show them!

"If you then, being evil, know how to give good gifts to your children, how much more will your Father who is in heaven give good things to those who ask Him!"

Jesus, Son of God (see Matthew 7:11)

Our greatest assignment is to experience the love of the Father and then represent Him in all we do as we live fully alive. Our lives are to demonstrate a partnership with a limitless and loving Father.

"When the LORD brought back the captivity of Zion, we were like those who dream [it seemed so unreal]. Then our mouth was filled with laughter, and our tongue with singing. Then they said among the nations, "The LORD has done great things for them." The LORD has done great things for us, and we are glad."

Psalm 126:1–2

"God be merciful to us and bless us, and cause His face to
shine upon us, that Your way may be known on earth,
your salvation among all nations. God shall bless us, and all
the ends of the earth shall fear Him."

Psalm 67:1, 2, 7

THE PROCESS OF DREAMING WITH GOD

So how do you partner or dream with God in business?

If all you do is focus on the benefits of having God with you, you
devalue the Person to a transaction. If you forget His benefits, you
devalue the relationship and hide who He really is from a world
that is starving to know His Nature. Through the pursuit of
knowing God the Father as your friend and growing in awareness
and expectation of what that friendship releases around you, your
ability to dream with Him will grow.

Remember, our relationship with Father God is even better than
having a billionaire philanthropist as your best friend. We must
dream bigger in order to live out our God-sized dreams and
demonstrate to the world a limitless and loving Father.

The following diagram shows the cycle of dreaming with God
and turning those dreams into reality. The first step is intimacy
with Him.

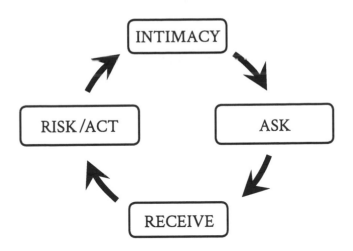

1. INTIMACY

The greatest privilege of humanity is to have a personal, experiential relationship with the Father of Creation. God sent his Son, Jesus, to fully demonstrate what the Father looked like and to show what we can accomplish when we are in a relationship with Him. The closer you get to Him, the more His life spills over into yours. You become like what you worship or behold (what you think on most often). So set your heart to seek Him. Spend time in His Presence. Make a priority of focusing on Him and being with Him. Set aside time to create with Him.

What is holding you back from experiencing a greater measure of friendship with Father God?

How could you adjust your schedule to involve more of Him in your life?

Would your friends and family describe friendship with God as important in your life? What will you do about that?

2. ASK, DREAM, IMAGINE, AND CREATE

As you build a deeper friendship with the Father, take time to ask—to dream with Him.

Find a place and time that works for you to be still, without distraction. That may be with a cup of coffee in your hand sitting in your favorite café or alone in the woods surrounded by nature.

Direct your thoughts towards Heaven and experience His Presence with you.

Meditate on who He is: the God of all creation who fashioned the heavens with his fingers and set the stars in their place, who created the earth to be inhabited and chooses to dwell with people.

Meditate on who He says you are. Consider what He wants to say to you through Mark 1:11 and Luke 15:31: "You are my beloved son/daughter, in whom I am well pleased." "Son/Daughter, you are always with Me and all I have is yours." Let go of the obstacles, restraints and limitations that you are acutely aware of because of past experiences.

From the awareness that God is with you and that you are seated with Christ in Heavenly realms (see also Ephesians 2:6), where there is no limitation or lack, begin to ask Him the following questions. As you ask, don't get distracted by jumping to HOW you could do it. Just dream with Him:

- What is Your dream for me? How do You see me? What do You feel when you think of me?

- What is Your dream for my business? How do You feel about my business? What does a partnership with God in my business look like?

- What is Your dream for my city? How do You want to release Heaven through my business?

3. RECEIVE

As sons and daughters of Father God, we get to live from inheritance rather than having to earn something. This doesn't mean you sit back and wait for Him to do everything—your part is coming next, but Jesus paid full price for your full freedom and entry into abundant life. You cannot earn or make a payment for what He has freely given. You cannot earn a gift. This is not about your performance; it's about His partnership with you. In order to access the God-dreams for you and your business, you need to receive what He is giving you.

Say out loud: "I am a generous receiver; I receive all that Jesus paid for, in full."

Go back over Step 2, asking and creating and imagining with God again. What if you truly believed God were WITH YOU—what would you do? What would your life, your business, your dreams look like if they were "God-sized"?

4. RISK—DO IT

Now it's time to do something. This is where you get to put your skin in the game and take the risk to turn the ideas and dreams you have just identified, into practical action steps.

Often the ideas will be large and sometimes overwhelming compared to where you are right now—that's the invitation into dreaming with a limitless God. Remember, "God didn't first call you to accomplish some great task for Him; He first called you to be with Him" (Bill Johnson). Success is a journey, not a destination. The more you can celebrate and enjoy the journey with God, the greater your overall success will be.

"Discovering and fulfilling your dreams is a journey, an adventure with God, so relax and enjoy the ride!" - *Dream Culture*

To turn your dream into an action step, consider the story of feeding the 5,000 in Mathew 14:15–21. The task was impossible given the resources, location and absence of any plan. But the disciples were given a clear intended outcome and a mandate to make it happen: "You feed them."

Is it possible they could have done anything—summoned a flock of quail, rained down manna and accessed water from a rock?

Jesus didn't say *how* they were to feed the multitude of hungry customers. Who said they needed something to start with? The One who gave the command to do it was the same One who made the world from nothing—simply by speaking it into being. But the disciples were not ready for that, so Jesus simplified it by giving them some clues. "What *do* you have?" Initially they had focused on what they *didn't* have. They then discovered and brought the little they did have, gave it to Jesus, who gave thanks, and started the most successful distribution network the world has ever seen. No fanfare, loud angel cries or deep intercessory groaning, just a practical action partnered with a supernatural God through thanksgiving. It would have been so effortless; it usually is. But they kept distributing and distributing and distributing! And then the kicker: they gathered up more at the end than what they started with.

So how do you do the impossible; how do you partner with God to move towards an impossible dream?

First, know your intended outcome. What does success look like? How will you know you have achieved your dream? Imagine a future date, living in the fulfillment of your dream. What does the day involve? Be specific. When will this be?

Now what do you want to start with? What is in your hand? What are the resources you may have access to right now? Who could you talk to? What is one thing you will do this week to partner with God and move towards your dream? Take that action step and give thanks to God for it, regardless of how big or small it may seem. Now do it!

Once you have made the first step, do the same again: take another step, and another, and another.

> **"Take the first step in faith. You don't have to see the whole staircase. Just take the first step."**
>
> *Martin Luther King Jr.*

For more practical steps on dreaming with God, see *Dream Culture: Bringing Dreams to Life* by Andy and Janine Mason.

SUMMARY *Dreaming with God*

• "Christ in me" is the greatest competitive advantage of any disciple of Jesus in business. "Christ in me" is the demonstration of absolute power governed by absolute love.

• According to God's standard of abundant living, principles alone will leave you short-changed.

• Any time we reduce our covenant with God to a set of rules, we miss the whole point of why Christ came to earth.

• You have permission to dream with God. You have permission to access the fullness of the covenant partnership you signed up for in making Christ your Lord.

• The single greatest vacuum in the world is the knowledge of the nature of God as Father. The nature of God as Father is not fully revealed in meeting needs but in meeting desires— dreams of the heart!

• When we live our dreams with God, life is released, our joy is made manifest and we show the world how good our Father God is.

• Our greatest assignment is to experience the love of the Father and then represent Him in all we do as we live fully alive.

• The process of dreaming with God starts and ends with intimacy—intimate friendship with Father God.

APPLICATION *Dreaming with God*

Go back over the action steps outlined earlier in this chapter. Below is a brief summary. You can also access a more detailed process to dreaming with God through the *Dream Culture* book or through our website, andyandjanine.com.

1. Increase your intimacy with God as Father and friend. You have permission to dream, to create and to explore. It is in dreaming and living your dreams that you reveal to the world the nature of God as loving and limitless Father. How could you develop your relationship with Him? What questions could you ask Him? How will you prioritize connection with Him?

2. Find a place that works for you to be still, without distraction. Begin to ask the Father questions about His dreams with you and for you.

3. Receive. What might Father God want to give you that you are trying to earn? Are you approaching Him as loving Father or benevolent boss? Revisit your dream list in light of a refreshed understanding as a son or daughter of a Father God, living from inheritance. God-size your dreams.

4. It's time to do something—take a risk and make an action step towards your dream. Sharpen your focus. How will you know you have achieved your dream? What will that look like, feel like, and sound like? Now, what *could* you do to move towards your dream? What do you *want* to do? What *will* you do? When?

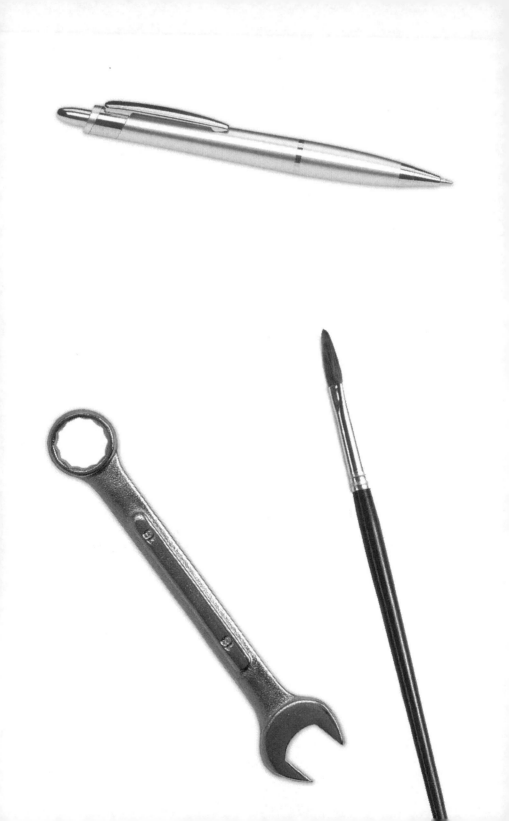

Supernatural Keys of Success

**And they overcame him by the blood of the Lamb
and by the word of their testimony, and they did not
love their lives to the death.**

Revelation 12:11

If you knew you had access to a set of tools and paradigms that had verified power to release increase in your business, would you not use them? The answer is fairly obvious, but sadly most of us have not accessed or applied the resources we have at our disposal. We have been happy to quote scripture and develop character, not realizing there is a whole realm of power we can tap into.

So what are some of the keys to access a demonstration of Heaven in your life and business? Revelation 12:11 loudly displays three of them: an experiential understanding of what Jesus did at the cross, remembering and repeating what Jesus has done in your life and the lives around you (past and present), and redefining success by what you can do for others rather than for yourself.

1. BY THE BLOOD OF THE LAMB
What Jesus did at the cross.

The first supernatural key to succeed in life and business is accessing what Jesus did on the cross for you. This is an experiential understanding that Jesus' blood didn't just deal with your sin, shame and brokenness. His blood restored *all things*; His blood bought *complete victory*; His blood brought you back into *right relationship as a child of God*. And the greatest thing is that all you do to start to experience the power of His blood is to acknowledge your need of Him, believe He is the Son of God, your Savior, Lord and King, and receive what He paid for in full—forgiveness, restoration of relationship, power and authority. He truly is better than we think!

If it is not present in Heaven, then it is not legal on earth.

When we understand what Jesus did was full and final, we get to walk in complete victory, and we no longer accept average. We no longer accept "impossible." We no longer accept "normal." We get to create life on earth from Heaven's perspective. If it is not present in Heaven, then it is not legal on earth (see Matthew 6:10). There is no sickness in Heaven, no oppression and no injustice. Heaven's streets are made from gold; there is no poverty or lack. Jesus empowered His followers to release His Kingdom, the Kingdom of Heaven, on earth. Everywhere you go, you can know that His will is "On earth as it is in Heaven." *You* are the enforcer of Heaven on earth.

You are the enforcer of Heaven on earth.

AJ had a background as an Occupational therapist in Germany. She would regularly have clients experiencing what we would call encounters with God during their therapy sessions.

While AJ was doing a Heaven in Business internship, she established a friendship with one of the local city officials.

One day she was visiting this city official to drop off a gift. The official was clearly unsettled about something, so she inquired about what was going on. He shared that his father had been diagnosed with leukemia and was not expected to live beyond four months. She immediately responded by saying she had a problem with anyone dying from disease because Jesus paid for that not to happen (Jesus' blood heals every sickness and disease). She then told him a testimony of another person being healed from cancer and offered a quick, 30-second prayer for the official's father.

The next week she heard back that the official's father had gone in for follow-up tests, and the doctors could no longer find the leukemia!

Another local businessman has a boutique winemaking business. One day he returned to his wine cellar, where a new batch of freshly made wine was in the fermentation process. He recognized by the smell that harmful bacteria had gotten into the wine and was destroying it. His immediate faith-filled response was to put his hand into the stainless steel vat of fermenting wine and pray for healing of the wine. And Jesus turned the bad wine into good wine!

What Jesus did on the cross was full and final. His blood paid for everything. Regardless of what messes or mistakes you have made in the past, you can approach His throne of grace, receiving the cleansing power of His blood in your life *and* into your business. But not only that—knowing the power of His blood and that your life is hidden in Christ, the same power that raised Jesus from the dead lives in you! (See Romans 8:11.) Through what He has done, you get to access power over sin, sickness and death. He is not limited to a Sunday pulpit or a priestly title; when you signed up to follow Christ, He promised these signs would follow *you!* (See Mark 16:17, 18.)

How does knowing Jesus' death and resurrection was all encompassing challenge or change the way you face life? What do you currently accept as "normal" that is actually a lie empowering a sub-standard life?

2. BY THE WORD OF YOUR TESTIMONY
What God has done in, through and around you and others.

The second supernatural key to succeed in life is remembering and repeating what God has done in and around you. You are part of a global family in Christ, so *any* testimony you hear is also yours by legal association. You just need to hear it and own it (repeat it until you see it happen in your own life or those around you).

Whenever you talk about what God is doing or has done, He cannot help but show up and "do it again." As Revelation 19:10 states, "The testimony of Jesus is the spirit of prophecy." It's even amazing that the place where God chose to dwell during the old covenant was a box that was also called the Ark of the *Testimony*.

Whenever you talk about what God is doing or has done, He cannot help but show up and "do it again."

"And there I will meet with you" (see Exodus 25:21). When you recall and repeat what He has done or is doing, He shows up and releases the power for it to happen again. He inhabits His testimony (see Psalm 22:3). When His Presence shows up, you cannot lose!

During one summer vacation, we got to stay in a lake house owned by a retired corporate manager. A couple of days before we arrived, the 62-year-old owner slipped between the back of his boat and the dock and damaged his rotator cuff (shoulder). He had an MRI and was waiting for the follow-up doctor's visit and report. His arm was in a sling, and he had excruciating pain if he raised it more than 45 degrees. We offered to pray for him and told a testimony of someone else's rotator cuff being healed and prayed, "Jesus, do it again." From this short prayer, he had a slight increase in movement before he again experienced restricting pain. We stood there repeating testimonies of Jesus healing other people's body parts—fractured foot, metal in wrist, carpal tunnel and tendonitis. Irrespective of the fact that none of these testimonies were for a torn rotator cuff, the Presence of God showed up just the same. After telling each testimony, we would ask him to check out his mobility, and each time he could lift his arm higher. Over about 15 minutes of storytelling and testing, his mobility increased and pain reduced to such an extent that he could rotate his arm fully around over his shoulder. He only mentioned slight stiffness. He immediately removed the sling and set it aside—it was no longer necessary. When we recalled and repeated the testimony of Jesus, He showed up and did it again!

Jeremiah and Shellie own a pizza company. Every day for the last year, they had prayed as they prepared the pizza dough. They declared that when people ate the pizza, they would experience wholeness, healing, restoration and joy, being overwhelmed by the Presence of God.

Molly was a local childcare worker in her 20s and had been lactose intolerant as a child. In December of the previous year, she had found out she could not eat lactose (dairy) or gluten and that she shouldn't eat corn products either. Over the following eight months, she had a series of night dreams in which she ate food containing gluten or dairy. In the dream she would always spit out the food but was left with an anxious feeling that she was about to get sick.

Molly had received prayer for these issues on a number of occasions but said, "I avoided it [prayer] because I felt an unspoken pressure to test it afterwards. I felt so terrible if I accidentally ate a little gluten or dairy; I didn't want to do it on purpose."

Then in September, Molly had a dream in which she was eating pizza from the company that Jeremiah and Shellie ran (she did not know them). In the dream she knew she was healed because in all the other dreams, she was still sick.

The next day, Molly told some Christian co-workers about the dream and her desire to test it out. She also said to them that she was a little nervous because it was a very busy workweek, and she didn't have time to get sick (if she was not healed).

One of Molly's coworkers told her about someone she knew who had been healed of food allergies after eating pizza from that company. This testimony released faith, and Molly was sold on "going for it."

The next evening, Molly purchased a medium sized pizza with a bunch of toppings and ate most of it. As Molly says, "I used to have my skin break out and itch even from just a little bit of gluten within 24 hours of having eaten it, and I would have extreme pain in my stomach within hours of having even a trace of cheese. According to my doctor, if I ate the amount of gluten and dairy that I ate that week, I would 'feel like I got hit by a truck.' I've been fine! No pain, no skin issues, nothing—now for two months!"

When the Israelites held onto their testimony, remembering and telling it to the next generation, they won. Hezekiah was a remarkable king who remembered and restored Israel's covenant with God and reminded the people who they really served. When surrounded and outnumbered by the most powerful army on earth, Hezekiah encouraged His people to trust God, saying, "There are more with us than with him [enemy]. With him is an arm of flesh; but with us is the Lord our God, to help us and to fight our battles" (see 2 Chronicles 32:6–8, 20–21). God then sent an angel, who cut down every mighty man of valor, leader and captain in the enemy camp. The enemy was forced to withdraw, shamefaced to their own land.

Nehemiah was another example of remembering the testimony and accessing a supernatural power to overcome. Not only did he remind the people (see Nehemiah 1:18; 4:14), he also reminded God of His promises to His people (see Nehemiah 1:8). Nehemiah started out in the hospitality industry serving the King of Babylon. He was then appointed by the king to lead a ragtag bunch of exiles from Babylon back to Israel to rebuild the broken-down city walls of Jerusalem. He faced opposition from the overwhelming task at hand, attempted hostile takeovers, false accusation, political manipulation and corrupt leaders. Yet through all this, he continued to remember God, remind the people of what God had already done and declare to them what He would do again.

In the end, Nehemiah and the people took only 52 days to rebuild the entire city walls. "And it happened, when all our enemies heard of it, and all the nations around us saw these things, that they were very disheartened in their own eyes; for they perceived that this work was done by our God" (Nehemiah 6:15, 16).

When the Israelites forgot the works of God, they forsook His ways and began losing. Psalm 78 describes this in blazing clarity, saying the children of Ephraim, though fully equipped for war, turned back in the moment of conflict because they "forgot His works and His wonders that He had shown them" (see Psalm 78:9–11).

How often have we turned back in our own moments of conflict or challenge because we have forgotten what He has already done for us in the past?

How often have we turned back in our own moments of conflict or challenge because we have forgotten what He has already done for us in the past? What He has done in the past He will do again for us if we hold fast to His covenant by remembering and repeating "His-story."

Bethel Church's pastoral staff has a two-hour weekly meeting. The first one and a half hours of this time is spent repeating testimonies of what Jesus is doing all over the world. We then pray over specific requests and spend the last 10–15 minutes going around the room updating current activities and schedules. Historically the majority of the testimonies repeated have to do with healing miracles. More recently we have been intentionally repeating testimonies of what Jesus is doing in the marketplace—in business, in government, in education. As we have intentionally repeated testimonies of financial increase, divine ideas and business development, the number and influence of these testimonies has increased. We get more of what we repeat. If you want specific testimonies to start manifesting in your life, intentionally collect those testimonies from others and then make excuses to repeat them. What is it that you want breakthrough in?

We get more of what we repeat.

One of the areas we have been targeting in prayer and in testimony is supernatural business increase that comes as a direct result of releasing His Presence—"Peace to this house" (see Luke 10:5-6). Business typically rises and falls on confidence, and peace undergirds confidence. The opposite of this is anxiety or fear. With this in mind, we took a team of 21 students from the Heaven in Business track at Bethel and went to the New York Stock Exchange. Everywhere we went on the trading floor, the podium, and even the boardroom, we intentionally released the Presence of God, declaring "Peace to this house" (without drawing any attention to ourselves).

We were invited to pray for individuals, who received prophetic words, encouragement, refreshing and a general increase in hope. At the same time, the Dow Jones broke out of its slowly rising plane to reach record highs three days in a row. The USA Today reported "...the Dow's revival." [1] CNN Money reported, "All three indexes had one of their best weeks of the year... there hasn't been any one catalyst pushing stocks higher lately." [2] Is it possible that our greatest advantage truly is His Presence?

A few weeks after returning from New York to California, we got to take another team into a local business that was expanding their premises. In the process, they were concerned about the higher overhead and staffing requirements involved. We repeated some testimonies of what God had been doing in business and then walked throughout the building releasing "Peace to this house." As we were about to leave, the CEO received a phone call from one of his staff. He intently listened, then asked the staff person to repeat what he just said so he could put it on speakerphone. We all heard that the company had just been contacted by a business requesting a quote on 25–100 mechanical panels per month. When we asked what this meant, the CEO replied, "Currently we are doing 3–5 per YEAR!" He ended the call and said, "This is stupid," with a big grin on his face. Next, he busted out his "happy dance" moves. "I'm going back to the office and they will all know—they knew what we were doing over here. Some of them will say, 'That is *so* God.' Others will be thinking, 'That is spooky.'"

When you read this testimony, what do you experience? How often do you recall what He has done in your life and the lives of those around you?

One night recently, I was heading to bed and feeling anxious about so many things. I consciously turned my thoughts to a testimony that I had heard that day:

117

A three-year-old boy visited his Grandma. She said to her grandson, "Grandma can't play with you today because she is not feeling well; you will have to play on your own." A few moments later, he returned and said, "Jesus can heal you." Grandma said, "You are right, you can pray for me." The family of the three-year-old only prayed before meals and at bedtime. With this in mind, he put his hand on his Grandma and prayed, "Thank you Jesus for the food." Grandma felt instantly healed and was then able to play with him!

After meditating on this, I started to say, "Thank you Jesus for the food...!" It's amazing how changing what your mind is fixed on changes everything. After thinking on the words of this testimony, my heart and spirit aligned, peace returned and anxiety left.

What if you chose to fast from (avoid) bad news for a month and instead fed yourself on a piece of good news every day?

What if you chose to fast from (avoid) bad news for a month and instead fed yourself on a piece of good news every day? What if you repeated this good news to yourself and to those around you? What could you do to record your own stories of God in your business and spread those around intentionally seeking God to "meet with us here" and "do it again"?

3. BY LIVING SELFLESSLY
What you are prepared to do for others.

The third supernatural key to succeed in life and business is shifting your definition of success from yourself to others. When you shift your focus from your own individual needs and desires to focusing on His Kingdom advancing, you become impossible to beat. Winning becomes something far greater than owning your own home, having a successful career or growing the biggest business. Winning becomes His Kingdom advancing.

More specifically, this looks like putting people before profit and investing in individuals more than architecture. Your employees, colleagues and clients are more than a number or a revenue source; they are made in the image of the Father and uniquely represent Him in some way. As soon as we lose sight of people's inherent value, we begin to take them for granted and lose traction in building in a way that reflects our Creator.

God has put a different talent in each of us that enables us to do this, but when you seek His Kingdom first, He then has the habit of adding to you everything you need and more! (See Matthew 6:33.)

We left a lot behind when we came from New Zealand to Redding, California. We couldn't deny God was speaking, but we certainly couldn't see how it would work out. Five years later, we are amazed at what He is unfolding. It's not always pain free, but the benefit is so much greater than we could ever have imagined. We gave Him pebbles, and He gives us back diamonds in exchange!

Just before last summer, I was doing a Dream presentation, and a businessman asked me afterwards what one of my personal dreams was. I said it was to take my family on vacation—maybe a long weekend away in Sacramento, visiting the zoo and hanging

---

As soon as we lose sight of people's inherent value, we begin to take them for granted and lose traction in building in a way that reflects our Creator.

---

out together. He started asking questions like, "Do they enjoy water? Do they like boating?" I said "Absolutely." Next thing I know, he offered us his family holiday home, plus all our flights and expenses—and access to a boat, a jet ski and other fun toys for our family for a week.

When we put His Kingdom first, He added back to us more than we could ever imagine!
Bless the LORD, O my soul, and forget not all His benefits!

How has God added benefits to you as you have pursued His dream?

What can you do this week to elevate the status of people around you and promote their dreams?

References:

1. USA Today Article:
   http://www.usatoday.com/story/money/markets/2013/04/
   09/stocks-bull-market-easy-money/2069423/

2. CNN Money:
   http://money.cnn.com/2013/04/12/investing/
   stocks-markets/index.html

SUMMARY *Supernatural Keys of Success*

- We have been happy to quote the scripture and develop the character, not realizing that there is a whole realm of power we can tap into.

- The first supernatural key to succeed in life and business is accessing what Jesus did on the cross for you—an experiential understanding that Jesus' blood didn't just deal with your sin, shame and brokenness; His blood restored *all things*; His blood bought *complete victory*; His blood brought you back into *right relationship as a child of God.*

- If it is not present in Heaven, then it is not legal on earth (see Matthew 6:10). *You* are the enforcer of Heaven on earth.

- The second supernatural key to succeed in life is remembering and repeating what God has done in and around you. You are part of a global family in Christ, so *any* testimony you hear is also *yours* by legal association.

- When you recall and repeat what He has done or is doing, He shows up and releases the power for it to happen again. He inhabits His testimony. When His Presence shows up, you win!

- The third supernatural key to succeed in life and business is shifting your definition of success from yourself to others. Winning becomes the advancement of His Kingdom, and you become impossible to beat. Love always wins.

- As soon as we lose sight of people's inherent value, we begin to take them for granted and lose traction in building in a way that reflects our Creator. When you seek His Kingdom first, He then has the habit of adding to you everything you need and more! (See Matthew 6:33.)

APPLICATION *Supernatural Keys of Success*

1. Overcome by the blood of the lamb. Start to experience the power of His blood by acknowledging your need of Him. Now confess Him as the Son of God, your Savior, Lord and King, and receive what He paid for in full—forgiveness, restoration of relationship, power and authority. Say out loud, "Jesus, I need you. I recognize you as the Son of God and confess you as my Savior, Lord and King. Forgive me for living less than what you have freely made available for me. I receive everything you paid for. Let the fullness of what you paid for manifest in my life and business. Thank you Father for restoring all things through Christ. Thank you that the same Spirit that raised Jesus from the dead lives in me."

2. Overcome by the word of your testimony. Remember, record and repeat what God has already done around you and others. How has He already provided for you, protected you, given you ideas and favor? How else has He shown up for you and for others? If you want specific testimonies to start manifesting in your life, intentionally collect those testimonies from others and then make excuses to repeat them. What is it that you want breakthrough in?

3. What if you chose to fast from (avoid) bad news for a month and instead fed yourself on a piece of good news every day? What if you repeated this good news to yourself and to those around you? What could you do to record your own stories of God in your business and spread those around, intentionally seeking God to "do it again"?

4. Overcome by living selflessly. How do people around you experience you at work, at home and at play? Do you know the dreams of your spouse, your family, your coworkers or your employees? What could you do this week to elevate the status of people around you and promote their dreams? How well are you representing the Father to them in your words, attitudes and actions? Where have you been living for yourself rather than living to elevate others? What will you do this week to demonstrate that God, who is love, is with you at work?

BONUS TESTIMONY
Multiplication of Wood Chips

With over 23 years' experience in his industry, **Chris** is a wood chip buyer for a particular energy company. The company's 50 MW power plant uses around 1,400 tons of wood chips per day.

After being with this particular company for a year, Chris had the opportunity to go with his wife on a 16-day mission trip. The problem was he would need to ensure the plant did not run out of wood chips while he was away. Secondly, the timing of the trip (March) coincided with the most difficult month to access a supply of chips. In spite of this, Chris's manager approved the time off.

The January and February leading up to the mission trip were exceptionally dry months, resulting in what Chris called "a super abundant supply." By the time he left on the trip, there were enough wood chips in the plant's storage to provide for 16 more days than Chris had planned!

Wood chip deliveries dropped dramatically while Chris was gone, and by the time he returned, the wood chip inventory was noticeably down. Chris began to lose sleep worrying about where he would find enough wood chips to keep the plant going. He complained to God, "If the plant runs out of fuel, then my manager will never let me go on a mission trip again."

Chris told his wife about his concerns, asking her to pray. She suggested he take some plastic gold coins and scatter them over the chip pile as a prophetic act declaring that God, as abundant provider, would multiply the chips in the piles.

It took Chris a few days, but finally he mustered up the courage to follow through on his wife's God-idea. One afternoon in mid-April, he stood by the side of the conveyor, carrying wood chips to the pile with a pocket full of gold coins. He began dropping coins one at a time on the moving conveyor declaring, "God is my provider. He did not pave the way for me to go to Ecuador to see me fail now. He is worthy to be trusted. He promised to supply all my needs and bless me to be a blessing to my employer."

Then things started to happen!

First, in early May a survey company was employed to accurately assess the quantity of chips in the pile (for inventory). The survey showed there were 7,000 tons MORE than what the books showed! For the next two months, Chris noticed that even when the chip piles should have been shrinking, they seemed to remain the same size.

Another survey was performed in early July that showed there were now 16,000 additional tons in the piles than what showed on the books! Although there were some minor efficiency repairs made to the boilers in May, this did not account for the magnitude of difference between actual and book inventory.

In response, the accountants adjusted the monthly chip use downward by 10 percent to try to get the book inventory closer to actual. At the end of two months, it seemed the chip piles were still growing faster than was being shown on the books, and the accountants further adjusted the monthly chip use downward by 15 percent for another three months.

In mid-December, the survey company returned to measure the piles. The report showed there were still 14,000 tons more than what was on the books—equivalent to an additional $720,000!

The magnitude of God's supernatural blessing to Chris' employer resulted in a direct bottom line profit increase of $1.5 million for the year. This was in addition to the inventory increase of $720,000 of unaccounted-for chips.

A physical inventory taken at the end of February showed the actual and book inventory were finally in balance. The $720,000 of unaccounted-for chips was accounted as profit for the new year. As Chris says, "All in all, God answered my gold coin prophetic act and extravagantly added $2.2 million worth of chips to my employer's income statement over a 10-month period. I now know that I need never worry about chip supply ever again because God continues to show that He is my abundant provider!"

RECOMMENDED RESOURCES

I personally recommend the following resources in assisting you on your journey to partner with God in your place of work. In addition, check out HeaveninBusiness.com for other recommended material.

BUSINESS AS CALLING
Anointed for Business, Ed Silvoso
Kingdom Economics, Paul Cuny

IDENTITY AND SONSHIP
Healing the Orphan Spirit, Lief Hetland
Experiencing the Father's Embrace, Jack Frost

HOSTING GOD
Hosting the Presence, Bill Johnson
Adoration Prayer Book, Bob Hartley

HEARING GOD
You May All Prophesy, Steve Thompson
Hearing from God (CD/MP3), Bill Johnson

LIVING FROM REST
The Hard Work of Rest, Stephen Graves
Rest(less), Rick Sbrocca

THE JOURNEY FROM PERFORMANCE TO PARTNERSHIP

Me, Myself, and Bob, Phil Vischer

Prosperity With Purpose, Mike Frank

THE NORMAL BELIEVER'S LIFE OF MIRACLES

When Heaven Invades Earth, Bill Johnson

The Supernatural Ways of Royalty, Kris Vallotton

Co-Labor Training (DVD/CD), Blake & Linda Schellenberg

PARTNERING WITH GOD AND LIVING YOUR DREAMS

Dreaming with God, Bill Johnson

Dream Culture, Andy & Janine Mason

Dream Journey (DVD/Workbooks), Andy & Janine Mason

CORRECTING WRONG MINDSETS

Cracks in the Foundation, Steve Backlund

Victorious Mindsets, Steve Backlund

FOREWORD BY DANNY SILK

DREAM
culture

bringing
dreams to life

ANDY & JANINE MASON

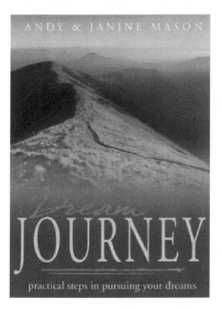

ANDY & JANINE MASON

JOURNEY

practical steps in pursuing your dreams

ABOUT THE AUTHOR

Andy Mason comes from New Zealand and since 1998 has been helping individuals and organizations discover and align with purpose, then develop practical steps to make dreams a reality. He has worked for a national consultancy firm and a leading financial institution and has invested in international community development.

Andy is the founder and director of Heaven in Business, a movement to connect and catalyze believers in the marketplace to partner with God in their realm of influence. This has led to the development of curriculum in Bethel's School of Supernatural Ministry, workshops and conferences, and a growing community of men and women in the marketplace who are distinguished from their colleagues by the tangible Presence of God.

Together with his wife, Janine, Andy also leads Dream Culture (andyandjanine.com), catalyzing people to discover and live their dreams. In 2011, they coauthored the book *Dream Culture: Bringing Dreams to Life*. Their Dream Journey DVD workshops are now being used in churches, schools and community centers around the world. Andy and Janine live with their four children in Redding, California.

Made in the USA
Lexington, KY
28 November 2019